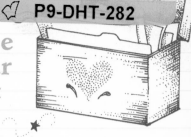

YOUR recipe could appear in our next cookbook!

Share your tried & true family favorites with us instantly at
www.gooseberrypatch.com
If you'd rather jot 'em down by hand, just mail this form to...
Gooseberry Patch • Cookbooks – Call for Recipes
2500 Farmers Dr., #110 • Columbus, OH 43235

If your recipe is selected for a book, you'll receive a FREE copy!

Please share only your original recipes or those that you have made your own over the years.

Recipe Name:

Number of Servings:

Any fond memories about this recipe? Special touches you like to add or handy shortcuts?

Ingredients (include specific measurements):

Instructions (continue on back if needed):

Special Code: **cookbookspage**

Over ➘

Extra space for recipe if needed:

Tell us about yourself...

Your complete contact information is needed so that we can send you your FREE cookbook, if your recipe is published. Phone numbers and email addresses are kept private and will only be used if we have questions about your recipe.

Name:
Address:
City: State: Zip:
Email:
Daytime Phone:

Thank you! Vickie & Jo Ann

Slow Cooking
All
Year'Round

Gooseberry Patch
2500 Farmers Dr., #110
Columbus, OH 43235

www.gooseberrypatch.com

1·800·854·6673

Do you have a tried & true recipe...
tip, craft or memory that you'd like to see featured in a **Gooseberry
Patch** cookbook? Visit our website at **www.gooseberrypatch.com**
to share them with us instantly. If you'd rather jot them down by hand,
use the handy form in the front of this book and send them to...

Gooseberry Patch
Attn: Cookbook Dept.
2500 Farmers Dr., #110
Columbus, OH 43235

Don't forget to include the number of servings your recipe makes,
plus your name, address, phone number and email address.
If we select your recipe, your name will appear right along
with it...and you'll receive a **FREE** copy of the cookbook!

Contents

Dedication

For all the creative cooks who know that
a comforting, home-cooked meal is never
out of reach any time of year, this one's for you!

Appreciation

A warm, hearty thank-you to all of
our Gooseberry Patch family who've
shared their all-time favorite
slow-cooker recipes with us.

Warming Winter Dishes

Christmas Egg Brunch

Amy Ott
Greenfield, IN

This is a wonderful breakfast dish for holiday guests. Simply put all your ingredients in the slow cooker before bedtime, turn it on and go to sleep. When you wake up, breakfast is cooked and ready to go!

6 to 8 slices bacon
32-oz. pkg. frozen hashbrowns
    with onions and peppers
1-1/2 c. shredded Cheddar
    cheese

1 doz. eggs
1 c. milk
1 t. dill weed
1/2 t. salt
1/2 t. pepper

In a skillet over medium heat, cook bacon until crisp; drain. Crumble bacon and set aside. Spray a slow cooker generously with non-stick vegetable spray. Place 1/3 of hashbrowns in slow cooker; top with 1/3 of bacon and 1/3 of cheese. Repeat layers twice more, ending with cheese. In a bowl, beat eggs, milk and seasonings. Pour over cheese. Cover and cook on low setting for 8 to 10 hours, until set. Serves 8 to 10.

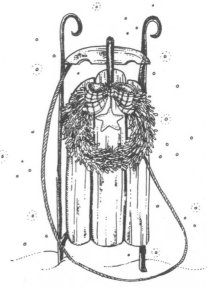

A basket of greenery on the seat
of an old rocking chair, a sled
leaning against the rail and
a pint-size evergreen in a
child's red wagon...a pretty
winter welcome for your porch!

Mom's Holiday Ham

Jennifer Snyder
Myerstown, PA

We started hosting the traditional Christmas morning breakfast when my family moved to a new home. My mom was buying too many presents to drag to the big family get-together! I make the eggs in the morning, and she slow-cooks a ham overnight. It's a delicious and easy way to start the day.

3-lb. boneless cooked ham   ground cloves to taste
1/2 c. water

Place ham in a slow cooker; pour water over top. Sprinkle with cloves. Cover and cook on low setting for 8 to 10 hours. Slice to serve. Serves 6 to 8.

Slow cookers are perfect when you're feeding a crowd!
Use several set on low to keep sausage gravy, scrambled
eggs or other breakfast foods warm and yummy
for Christmas brunch.

Brown Sugar Oatmeal

Stacey Korner
Wapwallopen, PA

I started hosting a Christmas Eve brunch a few years ago for some of our close friends. I've been making this easy oatmeal since the very first one...it's definitely a keeper!

1 c. steel-cut oats, uncooked
4 c. water
1/2 c. half-and-half
1/2 c. brown sugar, packed

2 T. vanilla extract
Optional: chopped dried fruit
 or nuts

Add oats, water and half-and-half to a slow cooker; stir well. Cover and cook on low setting for 4 to 5 hours. About 30 minutes before serving, stir in brown sugar, vanilla and fruit or nuts, if using. Serves 8.

Make lacy snowflakes for your windows! Gather pretty paper doilies, white poster paint and a sponge. Tape your doilies to a pane of glass, apply water-soluble paint with a sponge, then gently remove doilies. Best of all, these "snowflakes" wipe off with ease!

Warm Fruit Compote

Betty Lou Wright
Hendersonville, TN

It's a tradition in my family to have breakfast foods on Christmas Eve night. This easy and delicious warm fruit goes so well with our hashbrown casserole, grits and sausage bake.

29-oz. can sliced peaches, drained
20-oz. can pineapple chunks, drained
29-oz. can pear halves, drained
24-1/2 oz. jar mandarin oranges, drained
14-1/2 oz. jar spiced apple rings, drained
1/2 c. margarine, melted
24-oz. jar applesauce
3/4 c. brown sugar, packed
Garnish: cinnamon

Place fruit in a lightly greased slow cooker. In a bowl, combine margarine, applesauce and brown sugar; pour over fruit. Cover and cook on low setting for about 2 hours, until hot and bubbly. Before serving, sprinkle with cinnamon. Serves 10 to 12.

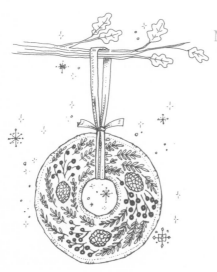

Make an ice wreath to hang from your outdoor tree branches... it will look so pretty sparkling in the sun! Just place greenery and some fresh cranberries inside a round gelatin mold, add about two inches of water and freeze. Fill the rest of the mold with water and freeze again. Remove wreath from mold and hang from a length of jute.

Cheesy Hashbrown Casserole

Tina Butler
Royse City, TX

Why not let your slow cooker help prepare this popular cheesy potato casserole? I adapted this recipe as a time and space-saver for the busy holiday season.

32-oz. pkg. frozen shredded
  hashbrowns
8-oz. container sour cream
10-3/4 oz. can cream of chicken
  soup

1/4 c. onion, diced
1-1/2 c. shredded Cheddar
  cheese
1/2 c. butter, melted
salt and pepper to taste

In a large bowl, combine all ingredients. Spoon mixture into a 4-quart slow cooker that has been sprayed with non-stick vegetable spray. Cover and cook on low setting for 4 to 5 hours, until hot and bubbly throughout and crisp on the sides. Serves 8.

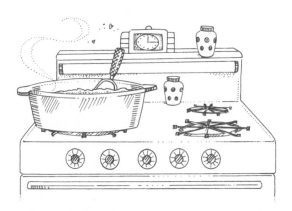

If a recipe calls for cooking a dish covered in the oven or on the stovetop for a long, low simmer, it can probably be converted to a slow-cooker recipe. Two to 4 hours of stovetop or oven cooking time will convert to 4 to 6 hours in the slow cooker on the high setting, or 7 to 9 hours on low. Layer root vegetables under meat and reduce the amount of liquid and seasonings used. Adjust seasonings toward the end of cooking time, if needed.

Warming Winter Dishes

Slow-Cooker Chai

JoAnn

*Your overnight holiday guests will love waking up to
this pleasing hot morning drink!*

3-1/2 qts. water
1/2 to 3/4 c. sugar
15 slices fresh ginger, peeled
36 whole cardamom seeds,
    pods discarded
25 whole cloves

5 4-inch cinnamon sticks
3 whole black peppercorns
8 black teabags
14-oz. can sweetened condensed
    milk

Pour water into a slow cooker. Stir in sugar and spices. Cover and cook
on high setting for up to 8 hours. Shortly before serving, steep teabags
in the hot liquid in the slow cooker for 5 minutes. Remove teabags;
strain whole spices. Stir in milk; serve hot. Serves 8 to 10.

Hot Buttered Rum

*Beth Bundy
Long Prairie, MN*

Perfect for holiday entertaining!

2 c. brown sugar, packed
1/2 c. butter
1/8 t. salt
4 4-inch cinnamon sticks
5 whole cloves

1/2 t. nutmeg
2 qts. hot water
2 c. rum
Garnish: whipped cream,
    nutmeg

Add brown sugar, butter, salt and spices to a slow cooker. Add hot
water. Stir well. Cover and cook on low for 5 hours. Add rum; stir.
Serve in warm mugs garnished with whipped cream and a sprinkle of
nutmeg. Makes about 2 quarts.

*Add a bit of sparkle and spice to holiday drinks...tie a little
ornament or bauble onto a cinnamon stick. The cinnamon
stick is a great stirrer, while the ornament dangles over your
mug of hot cocoa, mulled cider or creamy eggnog.*

Best-Ever Hot Cocoa

Crystal Faulkner
Asheboro, NC

My whole family looks forward to my special hot cocoa made in the slow cooker. Everyone who has tried this recipe swears it's the best ever, and I have to agree!

1-1/2 c. whipping cream
14-oz. can sweetened condensed
  milk

2 c. milk chocolate chips
6 c. milk
1 t. vanilla extract

Combine all ingredients in a slow cooker. Cover and cook on low setting for 2 hours, stirring occasionally. Ladle into mugs; serve warm. Serves 8 to 10.

The crackle of a warm, cozy fire brings everyone together.
Enjoy a simple dinner of roasted hot dogs or toasty
pie-iron sandwiches, then make s'mores and serve
mugs of warm spiced cider.

Hot Lemonade

Michelle Marberry
Valley, AL

Not medicine, but it sure feels good on a scratchy winter throat.

4 c. water
juice of 14 lemons, or
   3 c. lemon juice

2 c. sugar
1/4 c. honey
Garnish: cinnamon sticks

Combine all ingredients except garnish in a slow cooker. Cover and cook on low setting for 3 hours. Whisk well. Ladle into mugs; serve with cinnamon sticks for stirring. Makes 9 servings.

The leaves fall, the wind blows,
and the farm country slowly changes from
the summer cottons into its winter wools.

–Henry Beston

Chicken Pot Pie

Kimberly Adams
Tacoma, WA

Scoop into individual bowls and top with one or two
flaky biscuits warm from the oven.

32-oz. container chicken broth
2 10-3/4 oz. cans cream of
　chicken soup
2 c. milk
3 boneless, skinless chicken
　breasts, cooked and cubed

2 c. frozen peas and carrots
1 t. salt
1-1/2 t. pepper
1-1/2 t. curry powder

Put all ingredients in a 6-quart slow cooker; stir to blend. Cover and cook on low setting for 6 to 7 hours, until hot and bubbly. Serves 6 to 8.

Enjoy a springtime bouquet during winter's frosty days!
Fill a galvanized pail with pebbles, then tuck in a variety of
tulip, daffodil or hyacinth bulbs. Add just enough water to
barely cover the pebbles, keep watered, and in a few weeks
you'll have lots of springtime blossoms.

Tasty Tamale Pie

Vickie

It's so simple...authentic-tasting tamales without all the work! It's easy to double for a crowd too.

1 lb. ground beef
15-oz. can kidney beans,
   drained and rinsed
10-oz. can enchilada sauce
1-1/2 t. garlic powder
8-1/2 oz. pkg. corn muffin mix
1/3 c. milk

1 egg, beaten
2 T. butter, melted
1/2 c. shredded Cheddar cheese
Garnish: sour cream, additional
   shredded cheese, salsa,
   chopped tomatoes

In a skillet over medium heat, brown beef; drain and place in a slow cooker. Add beans, enchilada sauce and garlic powder; stir well. In a bowl, combine dry muffin mix with milk, egg and butter; stir until just mixed. Fold in cheese. Spoon batter mixture over beef mixture. Cover and cook on low setting for 5 hours, or until topping is cooked through and set. Garnish individual servings as desired. Serves 6.

Do your favorite slow-cooker recipes finish cooking a few hours before you get home? If your slow cooker doesn't have a timer setting, then you may want to think about preparing the ingredients the night before. If you refrigerate the filled crock overnight, it will take 2 to 3 hours longer to cook, which is perfect when you will be out & about all day!

Spicy Shredded Beef Tostadas

Nikki Judd
Charlotte, NC

I have four kids who all like to eat different things. This is one of the few recipes they unanimously agree on! If you don't like spicy food, just use one can of peppers in adobo sauce.

3 to 4-lb. beef chuck roast
salt and pepper to taste
1 to 2 T. canola oil
1 to 2 7-oz. cans chipotle
    peppers in adobo sauce
15-oz. can tomato sauce
1 t. ground cumin

1 t. coriander
1 t. garlic powder
2 t. dried, minced onion
tostadas or taco shells
Toppings: sour cream, shredded
    cheese, chopped tomatoes,
    shredded lettuce

Bring roast to room temperature; sprinkle with salt and pepper. Heat oil in a skillet over medium heat; add roast to skillet and brown on all sides. Place roast in a slow cooker. In a bowl, mix peppers with sauce, tomato sauce and seasonings. Pour mixture over beef. Cover and cook on low setting for 8 to 10 hours, or on high setting for about 6 hours. Shred roast with 2 forks; mix well with sauce in slow cooker. Serve on tostadas or taco shells, topped as desired. Serves 8 to 10.

Slow-cook a pot of creamy beans to serve with pork. Rinse and drain 1/2 pound dried navy beans. Place them in a slow cooker and stir in a chopped onion, a tablespoon of bacon drippings or butter and 5 cups boiling water. Cover and cook on high for 4 hours, stirring occasionally. Don't add salt until the beans are tender. So easy!

Chicken Adobo

Vicki Snyder
Santa Maria, CA

When I was a girl growing up in Guadalupe, a farming community along the central coast of California, my mom made me this wonderful dish every year for my birthday. She never wrote the recipe down, so after she passed away, I was never able to recreate it. But then I got this recipe from my friend's daughter-in-law. It's very much like the one my mom used to make. Serve over sticky white rice.

1 onion, sliced	1 c. white vinegar
7 to 8 cloves garlic, pressed	1 c. soy sauce
2 T. cracked pepper	cooked short-grain white rice
2 bay leaves	
3 to 3-1/2 lbs. chicken thighs and drumsticks	

Place onion in a slow cooker. Wrap garlic, pepper and bay leaves in cheesecloth and tie with kitchen string or place in a tea strainer. Add spice bundle to slow cooker. Add chicken. In a small bowl, mix vinegar and soy sauce. Pour over chicken. Cover and cook on low setting for 4 to 6 hours, stirring occasionally, until chicken juices run clear. Discard spice bundle before serving. Serve over rice. Serves 8.

Give Frosty a pair of rosy cheeks! Mix five drops red food coloring with a cup of water; pour into a spray bottle. Finely mist your snowman's cheeks for just the right touch of color.

Beef Stroganoff

Amy Wagner
Constantine, MI

*Serve over cooked rice or mashed potatoes instead of using noodles,
if you wish! You can also make a chicken version by substituting
four to six boneless, skinless chicken breasts for the beef.*

1-1/4 lbs. stew beef cubes
1-1/2 c. sour cream
10-3/4 oz. can cream of
   mushroom soup

1.35-oz. pkg. onion soup mix
16-oz. pkg. wide egg noodles,
   uncooked

Place beef in a slow cooker. In a bowl, combine sour cream, soup and
soup mix; spoon over beef. Cover and cook on low setting for 4 hours.
About 15 minutes before serving, cook noodles according to package
directions; drain and stir into beef mixture. Warm through. Serves 6.

For a warm, cozy holiday fragrance, simmer cinnamon sticks,
citrus peel, whole cloves and nutmeg in a mini slow cooker.
Just add 2 to 3 cups of water and set on low.

Easy Chicken à la King

Barbara Cebula
Chicopee, MA

I make this simple slow-cooker recipe whenever I'm on the go...it's so nice to come home to a hot meal. It's also tasty with some chopped green pepper, if you have one on hand.

1-1/2 lbs. boneless, skinless
   chicken breasts, cubed
10-3/4 oz. can cream of
   chicken soup
3 T. all-purpose flour

1/4 t. pepper
9-oz. pkg. frozen peas and
   onions, thawed and drained
2 T. chopped pimentos
1/2 t. paprika

Place chicken in a slow cooker. In a bowl, combine soup, flour and pepper. Spoon over chicken; do not stir. Cover and cook on high setting for 2-1/2 hours, or on low setting for 5 to 5-1/2 hours. About 20 to 30 minutes before serving, stir in remaining ingredients. Cover and cook on high setting for 20 to 30 minutes longer. Makes 4 servings.

Ropa Vieja de Cubano

Bren Rogers
Atwood, CA

This recipe is a favorite in our house! "Ropa vieja" translates literally to "old clothes," and the children in our family love to ask for old clothes for dinner.

2-lb. beef flank steak
10-oz. can diced tomatoes with
   green chiles
1 onion, diced
2 t. chili powder

1-1/2 t. ground cumin
1 t. dried oregano
1 bay leaf
2 c. salsa

Place steak in a slow cooker, trimming to fit if needed. Pour in tomatoes with juice; add remaining ingredients except salsa. Cover and cook on high setting for 3 hours, or on low setting for 6 hours, until steak is fork-tender. Shred steak using 2 forks. Stir in salsa. Cook, leaving lid slightly ajar, on high setting for 30 minutes longer, or until liquid has cooked down. Discard bay leaf before serving. Serves 8.

Tessie's Lazy Pierogie

Donnalynn Dennis
New Albany, IN

*I learned how to make this comfort-food dish from my grandmother.
Now I make it for family get-togethers and whenever I miss home...
I always think of Gramma's smile and her wise words. It's excellent
served with Kielbasa sausage.*

16-oz. pkg. kluski egg noodles,
   uncooked
1 onion, chopped
2 to 3 t. oil
14-1/2 oz. can sauerkraut,
   drained

sugar to taste
salt and pepper to taste
10-3/4 oz. can cream of
   mushroom soup
Optional: 1/2 c. milk

Cook noodles according to package directions, until just tender; drain
and place in a slow cooker. In a skillet over medium heat, sauté onion
in oil until translucent; add sauerkraut. Cook and stir until most of the
liquid is gone. Add sugar, salt and pepper to taste. Add onion mixture
to slow cooker; stir in soup. If desired, add milk for a creamier texture.
Mix well. Cover and cook on low setting for 3 to 4 hours, until heated
through. Serves 8 to 10.

For a simple winter centerpiece, arrange sparkly ornaments
on a cake stand, dust with glittery mica snow, then cover
with a glass cloche...charming!

4-Cheese Lasagna

Deedra Rogers
Booneville, AR

Since I have started making lasagna in the slow cooker, we eat it more often...the no-boil noodles make it so easy. I always use my largest slow cooker and a disposable liner. Clean-up is a cinch!

1 lb. lean ground beef
2 26-oz. jars chunky tomato,
    garlic & onion pasta sauce
1/2 c. water
1 T. Italian seasoning
salt and pepper to taste
2 T. grated Parmesan cheese

16-oz. container small-curd
    cottage cheese
8-oz. pkg. oven-ready lasagna
    noodles, uncooked
4 c. shredded mozzarella cheese
2 c. shredded Colby Jack cheese

In a skillet over medium heat, brown beef; drain and remove from heat. Stir in sauce, water and seasonings. In a bowl, combine Parmesan cheese and cottage cheese; set aside. In a large lightly greased slow cooker, spread some beef mixture; top with noodles, breaking them to fit in the slow cooker if needed. Top with some beef mixture, some cottage cheese mixture and some of both kinds of shredded cheese. Repeat layers 2 to 3 more times, ending with shredded cheese. Cover and cook on low setting for 3-1/2 to 4 hours, until noodles are tender. Turn off slow cooker; let stand for 10 minutes before serving. Serves 8 to 10.

A festive touch for your holiday table...a wreath of rolls! Arrange thawed dinner rolls in a ring on a parchment paper-lined baking sheet. Brush with butter, sprinkle with green herbs and bake as directed. Looks pretty on a cake stand!

Donna's Green Chile Stew

Donna Wilson
Chesapeake, VA

My husband grew up in New Mexico. Being a military family, we've since moved all over the place. I created this recipe for him so he could enjoy all the favorite flavors of his home state. It's a regular at our dinner table.

1 to 2-lb. boneless pork roast,
   cubed
1 onion, diced
1 T. oil
2 15-1/2 oz. cans white
   hominy, drained
28-oz. can green chile enchilada
   sauce

4-oz. can diced green chiles
2 to 3 cloves garlic, minced
2 potatoes, peeled and diced
2 carrots, peeled and thinly
   sliced
salt and pepper to taste
flour tortillas

In a skillet over medium heat, brown pork and onion in oil. Transfer to a large slow cooker; add remaining ingredients except tortillas. Mix well. Cover and cook on low setting for 6 to 8 hours. To serve, scoop mixture onto tortillas. Serves 8.

Need extra oven space? Try roasting veggies in the
slow cooker...you won't even need to add any water or oil!
The vegetables have enough of their own moisture
to cook properly. So simple!

Warming Winter Dishes

Vegetarian Mexican Chili

Laura Witham
Anchorage, AK

*I sampled this chili while visiting a friend of mine, and I loved it
so much I asked for the recipe! I make it whenever I need
an easy meal to feed a crowd.*

2 15-oz. cans ranch-style beans
2 10-oz. cans diced tomatoes
   with green chiles
15-1/2 oz. can white hominy,
   drained
15-1/2 oz. can golden hominy,
   drained

1-oz. pkg. ranch salad dressing
   mix
3 c. vegetable broth
Garnish: shredded Cheddar
   cheese, crushed tortilla chips

In a slow cooker, combine beans with liquid, tomatoes with juice and
remaining ingredients except garnish. Cover and cook on low setting
for 8 hours, or on high setting for 6 hours. Garnish as desired.
Serves 6 to 8.

Spend a winter evening baking homemade dog biscuits and
cat treats...your friends will be touched when you
remember their pets with a small holiday gift!

Sweet-and-Sour Beef

Ellie Brandel
Milwaukie, OR

This easy recipe is delicious on a cold day. I first made it in 1976 for my brother's wedding rehearsal dinner. It was a big hit, and a family favorite ever since! Serve on its own, or over rice or pasta.

2 lbs. stew beef cubes
2 T. oil
2 c. carrots, peeled and thickly
    sliced
2 onions, chopped
1 green pepper, chopped
20-oz. can pineapple chunks,
    drained and juice reserved

15-oz. can tomato sauce
1/2 c. vinegar
1/2 c. light molasses
1/4 c. sugar
2 t. chili powder
2 t. paprika
1 t. salt
Optional: 1/4 c. cornstarch

In a large skillet over medium heat, brown beef in oil; drain. Combine beef, carrots, onions, pepper and pineapple in a large slow cooker. Stir well. In the same skillet, combine remaining ingredients except cornstarch; cook and stir over medium heat until well blended and heated through. Pour over beef mixture in slow cooker, stirring to coat. Cover and cook on high setting for 4 hours, or on low setting for 6 to 7 hours. For a thicker sauce, about 15 minutes before serving, dissolve cornstarch in reserved pineapple juice. Stir into slow cooker; cook for 15 minutes longer, or until thickened. Serves 6 to 8.

A snowy winter afternoon is the
perfect time to browse seed
and plant catalogs and start
planning your flower and
vegetable gardens for spring.

Winter Nights Chowder

Alyce Dixon
Madison, WI

This soup was inspired by traditional Finnish potato and salmon soup. Because of the soup's (and my own) Scandinavian heritage, I named it after the Nordic festival of Winter Nights.

1/2 red onion, chopped
2 T. butter
salt-free herb blend to taste
2 to 3 redskin potatoes, cubed
2 c. cold water, divided
2 bay leaves
2 turnips, peeled and cubed
2 parsnips, peeled and cubed
1-1/2 c. baby carrots

1 turnip, peeled, cooked and
    mashed
1 baking potato, peeled, cooked
    and mashed
1 c. broccoli flowerets
16-oz. can kidney beans
16-oz. can butter beans
1 c. whipping cream or milk

In a skillet over medium heat, sauté onion with butter and herb blend until tender. Add redskin potatoes; sauté lightly. Transfer mixture to a large slow cooker. Return skillet to stovetop; increase heat to high. Pour one cup water into skillet. As the water comes to a boil, stir and scrape browned bits from the skillet using a spatula. Add remaining water; return to a boil. Pour water over mixture in slow cooker, adding more water to cover, if needed. Add bay leaves, uncooked turnips, parsnips and carrots. Cover and cook on high setting for one hour. About 30 minutes before serving time, add mashed turnip and potato, broccoli and beans with liquid; stir. About 10 minutes before serving time, stir in cream or milk. Add more herb blend if desired. Discard bay leaves before serving. Ladle into bowls to serve. Serves 6 to 8.

The first fall of snow is not only an event,
but it is a magical event.
–J.B. Priestley

Old-Fashioned Oxtail Soup

Janet Powell McKee
Manteca, CA

*If it's cold and blustery outside, you will be warm and satisfied
with our Grandma Nance's soup. It's a tradition for
Thanksgiving and Christmas eves at our house.*

2 lbs. beef oxtails, cut into
    serving-size pieces
1/2 c. onion, chopped
2 to 3 T. oil
1/2 c. red wine or beef broth
1/2 head cabbage, chopped
28-oz. can crushed tomatoes
4 c. tomato juice

4 c. water
2 T. salt
1 c. chopped vegetables, such
    as carrots, celery, onion and
    green beans
16-oz. pkg. frozen corn
16-oz. pkg. wide egg noodles,
    uncooked

In a skillet over medium heat, brown oxtails with onion in oil. Cook
and stir until onion is tender. Pour in wine or broth. Increase heat to
high; cook and stir, scraping browned bits from the skillet, until liquid
is boiling. Carefully transfer contents of skillet to slow cooker. Add
remaining ingredients except noodles. Cover and cook on low setting
for 8 to 9 hours, stirring occasionally. About 15 minutes before
serving, prepare noodles according to package directions; drain. Stir
into soup. Serves 8 to 10.

Root vegetables like potatoes, carrots and onions grow
tender and sweet with all-day slow cooking. Give sweet
potatoes and parsnips a try too...delicious!

Erin's Ham & Cheese Soup

Erin Ho
Renton, WA

It was a dark stormy evening driving home from work. I wanted something comforting and cozy for dinner and I thought, "Why haven't I ever made ham and cheese soup?" The wheels started turning, and I created this. The recipe has been shared among family & friends. Everyone who's tried it has been very satisfied!

1 red pepper, diced
1 white onion, diced
3 to 4 cloves garlic, minced
1 jalapeño pepper, finely
   chopped and seeds removed
3/4 lb. cooked ham, diced
2 10-3/4 oz. cans Cheddar
   cheese soup
2 10-3/4 oz. cans cream of
   potato soup
3 c. pasteurized process cheese
   spread, diced
8-oz. pkg. shredded Cheddar
   Jack cheese
4 c. milk
1 c. whipping cream
1 t. salt, or to taste
2 t. pepper
1 T. garlic herb seasoning

Combine all ingredients in a slow cooker; mix well. Cover and cook on low setting for 4 to 6 hours, or on high setting for 2 to 3 hours, until bubbly and cheese is melted. Serves 8 to 10.

A heartfelt Valentine's Day message! Butter bread slices and cut into heart shapes using mini cookie cutters. Bake at 425 degrees until crisp. Garnish filled soup bowls with toasts before serving.

Winter Steak Kabobs

Glenda Tolbert
Moore, SC

Toss everything in the slow cooker before you head out for your holiday shopping. Serve with a tossed salad and garlic bread when you get back! Who needs a grill?

1-lb. beef sirloin tip steak, cubed
2 14-1/2 oz. cans whole
    potatoes, drained
salt and pepper to taste
1 green pepper, sliced

1 onion, sliced
15-1/4 oz. can pineapple
    chunks, drained
18-oz. bottle barbecue sauce

Place steak and potatoes in slow cooker; sprinkle with salt and pepper. Add pepper, onion and pineapple; cover with barbecue sauce. Cover and cook on low setting for 6 hours, or high setting for 4 hours, until steak and vegetables are tender. Serves 2 to 4.

For a quick and yummy cheese sauce for veggies, combine one cup evaporated milk and 1/2 cup shredded cheese. Stir over low heat until smooth.

Dreaming of Summer
Melt-Away Ribs

Kristy Wells
Candler, FL

During the summer my husband usually gets "volunteered" to cook for various events. He has developed his own method for smoking mouthwatering ribs. My family dreams of these ribs in the winter, so I came up with a great slow-cooker adaptation. Here's to you, honey...hope it does yours justice!

2-lb. slab pork baby back ribs
4 c. apple cider
2 T. Greek seasoning
2 T. smoke-flavored cooking
   sauce

2 T. dried, minced onion
2 T. cornstarch
2 T. cold water

Section ribs by cutting along the bone with a very sharp knife to make individual ribs. In a large slow cooker, combine all ingredients except cornstarch and water. Cover and cook on high setting for 2 hours. Reduce heat to low; cook for one to 2 hours longer, until ribs are tender. Ladle 2 cups of liquid from the slow cooker into a small saucepan. Bring liquid to a boil over medium-high heat. In a small bowl, whisk together cornstarch and water; add to saucepan, stirring constantly until sauce thickens. Serve ribs with sauce spooned over top. Serves 6 to 8.

Place newly arrived Christmas cards in a vintage napkin holder, then take a moment every evening to share happy holiday greetings from family & friends over dinner.

Tasty Dipped Roast Beef

Marlene Murray
Spanish Fork, UT

This is the easiest fix-it-and-go recipe, great for a day of winter fun. Place in the slow cooker before you leave home, and the delicious aroma will welcome you back!

2 to 3-lb. beef rump roast
1 T. oil
10-3/4 oz. can cream of
   mushroom soup

4 cubes beef bouillon
sandwich buns or Texas
   toast bread

In a skillet over high heat, brown roast in oil on all sides. Place roast in a slow cooker. Pour soup over top; place bouillon cubes around roast. Cover and cook on low setting for 8 hours. Remove roast from slow cooker; let rest 5 minutes. Slice thinly; serve on buns or on Texas toast as open-face sandwiches. Use sauce from slow cooker for dipping. Serves 6.

For a crisp holiday scent, hollow out grapefruit and orange halves. Tuck a votive in the center of each and surround with fresh cranberries.

Amy's Beef Stew

Amy Hauck
Portland, OR

I put this recipe together one winter morning and had a wonderful hearty stew by dinner! My husband raves about it, and it's so good with bread or rice.

2 to 3-lb. beef chuck roast, cubed
2 turnips, peeled and cubed
2 rutabagas, peeled and cubed
1 Yukon gold potato, peeled and cubed

1 onion, cut into wedges
2 10-3/4 oz. cans of cream of mushroom soup
1.35-oz. pkg. onion soup mix

Place beef and vegetables in a slow cooker; stir to mix. In a bowl, combine soup and dry soup mix. Pour over mixture in slow cooker. Cover and cook on low setting for 8 to 10 hours. Serves 4 to 6.

Be sure all meats are thoroughly cooked! Slow cooker recipes that use raw poultry or beef should cook a minimum of three hours on high setting.

Turnip Green Soup

Christy Bonner
Bankston, AL

This is a warming soup for a cold winter day. Mix up a pan of delicious cornbread and you have a hearty meal!

1 lb. mild or hot ground pork
   sausage
1 c. onion, chopped
1-1/2 c. carrots, peeled and
   chopped
27-oz. can seasoned turnip
   greens
14-oz. can seasoned turnip
   greens

10-oz. can diced tomatoes with
   green chiles
2 15-oz. cans black-eyed peas,
   drained and rinsed
1 t. red pepper flakes
1/2 t. pepper

In a skillet over medium heat, brown sausage with onion and carrots. Transfer sausage mixture to a slow cooker; add greens, tomatoes with juice, peas and seasonings. Cover and cook on high setting for one to 2 hours. Serves 6 to 8.

Leftover bits of fabric can find new life as simple beverage charms. Trim fabric to a 4 to 5-inch strip and tie to a glass stem. Simply charming!

Cream of Cauliflower Soup

Paula Marchesi
Lenhartsville, PA

When I was growing up, my mom always served soup with our holiday meals. I loved her creamy cauliflower soup...warm, delicious and oh-so satisfying. This soup is partly my mom's recipe and partly mine. I feel like with each spoonful we're together again, if only for a moment.

1 head cauliflower, chopped
2 c. chicken broth
2 T. reduced-sodium chicken
    bouillon granules
2 c. half-and-half
2 c. milk
1 carrot, peeled and shredded
2 bay leaves
1/4 t. garlic powder
1/2 c. instant mashed potato
    flakes
1 c. shredded Monterey Jack
    cheese
1 c. shredded Cheddar cheese
Garnish: paprika or minced fresh
    parsley

In a large saucepan, combine cauliflower, broth and bouillon. Bring to a boil. Reduce heat, cover and cook for 20 minutes, or until cauliflower is tender. Mash cauliflower in saucepan. Transfer entire contents of saucepan to a 3-quart slow cooker. Stir in half-and-half, milk, carrot, bay leaves and garlic powder. Cover and cook on low setting for 3 hours. Stir in potato flakes; cook 30 minutes longer, or until thickened. Discard bay leaves. Cool slightly. Using an immersion blender, process soup until smooth. Stir in cheeses. Cover and cook until soup is heated through and cheese is melted. Garnish servings with paprika or parsley. Serves 8.

Don't blow your top! When blending hot liquids, be sure to remove the stopper from the top of your blender so steam pressure doesn't build up inside. After removing the stopper, cover the hole with a clean, folded kitchen towel to prevent a mess before blending.

Hearty Meatball Stew

Karen Swartz
Woodville, OH

Busy day ahead? Prepare the ingredients for this easy recipe the night before. For a special treat, serve it ladled into individual sourdough bread bowls.

1 lb. new potatoes, cubed
16-oz. pkg. baby carrots
1 onion, sliced
2 4-oz. cans sliced mushrooms, drained
16-oz. pkg. frozen meatballs

12-oz. jar beef gravy
14-1/2 oz. can Italian-seasoned diced tomatoes
3-1/4 c. water
pepper to taste
14-1/2 oz. can corn, drained

In a large slow cooker, layer all ingredients except corn in the order listed. Cover and cook on low setting for 8 to 10 hours. About one hour before serving, stir in corn. Serves 8.

Make spice-scented pine cones to heap in a bowl...so sweet-smelling. Simply dip pine cones in melted beeswax (old candle ends will work just fine!) and while still warm, roll them in ground cinnamon, cloves and nutmeg.

Grammam Phyllis's Italian Meatballs

Heather Eldredge
Langhorne, PA

*This quick & easy recipe has been handed down for generations.
As the cooks get busier, the recipe's been made easier.*

1 lb. ground beef
1/2 c. Italian-flavored dry bread crumbs
1 t. grated Parmesan cheese

2 eggs, beaten
3 26-oz. jars favorite spaghetti sauce
16-oz. pkg. spaghetti, uncooked

In a large bowl, combine beef, bread crumbs, cheese and eggs; mix well. Form beef mixture into one-inch balls. Place meatballs in a slow cooker; cover with sauce. Cover and cook on low setting for 8 to 10 hours. About 15 minutes before serving, prepare spaghetti according to package directions; drain. Ladle sauce and meatballs over individual servings of spaghetti. Serves 6 to 8.

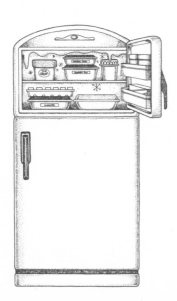

When cooking for Christmas, make use of your freezer. You can prepare soups weeks in advance and freeze them until you are ready to serve them, garnished with a swirl of fresh cream. They're an elegant yet simple appetizer for your holiday meal.

Ribs & Kraut

Christine Takada
Saint Paul, MN

This dish is a longtime family favorite, easily modified for different sized crowds. Just brown the ribs, put everything into the slow cooker, and you're free to enjoy your day and not worry about what's for dinner!

2 32-oz. pkgs. refrigerated
    Bavarian-style sauerkraut
4 to 6 potatoes, peeled and
    cubed
1 onion, cubed
1 t. caraway seed

2 to 4 lbs. boneless pork baby
    back ribs, cut into serving-
    size pieces
2 to 3 T. oil
1/4 c. brown sugar, packed
Optional: brown mustard

Add sauerkraut with juice, potatoes and onion to a 6-quart slow cooker; sprinkle with caraway seed and stir to mix. In a skillet over medium-high heat, brown ribs on both sides in oil. Add ribs to slow cooker, pushing them down into the sauerkraut mixture so ribs are immersed. Sprinkle brown sugar over all. Cover and cook on high setting for 5 to 6 hours, stirring occasionally, until ribs are fork-tender and potatoes are cooked through. To serve, ladle into shallow bowls or plates, making sure each serving contains some ribs, sauerkraut and potatoes. If you like, garnish each plate with a dollop of mustard on the side. Serves 4 to 6.

To make clean-up a breeze, lightly spray the inside of a slow cooker with non-stick vegetable spray before adding recipe ingredients. What a time-saver!

No-Fuss Sauerkraut & Pork

Gloria Kaufmann
Orrville, OH

This delicious, easy recipe from my daughter is great for a traditional German-inspired New Year's Day dinner. You can put your feet up and watch the Rose Bowl while dinner is cooking!

3-lb. boneless pork roast
32-oz. pkg. refrigerated
    sauerkraut, drained and
    rinsed
2 apples, peeled, cored and
    sliced

1/2 c. brown sugar, packed
1 c. apple juice
Optional: 1/2 to 1 t. caraway
    seed

Place roast in a large slow cooker; top with sauerkraut, apples and brown sugar. Pour juice over all and sprinkle with caraway seed, if using. Cover and cook on high setting for 4 to 5 hours, or low setting for 8 to 9 hours, until pork is fork-tender. Shred pork with 2 forks; combine with mixture in slow cooker before serving. Serves 8.

If your fireplace isn't used during the holidays, it can still look warm and inviting. Fill an empty grate with cheerful wrapped packages, candles of every shape and size or snowy white birch logs accented by shiny ornaments.

Red Beans & Rice

Beth Schlieper
Lakewood, CO

*My friend Sharon made this yummy dish for our family
about eight years ago, and I've made it ever since.
Tastes great served with a side of coleslaw!*

16-oz. Kielbasa sausage ring,
   sliced into bite-size pieces
4 to 5 15-oz. cans red beans,
   drained
2 14-1/2 oz. cans diced
   tomatoes

1 onion, chopped
hot pepper sauce to taste
salt, pepper and red pepper
   flakes to taste
cooked white rice

Place all ingredients except rice in a slow cooker. Mix well. Cover and
cook on low setting for 8 hours. Serve ladled over rice. Serves 8 to 10.

In southern Louisiana, it's traditional to serve King Cake
during the Carnival season. It's a cinnamon roll-like cake
topped with sugary icing tinted in the traditional Mardi Gras
colors of purple, green and gold. A trinket, such as a plastic
baby figurine, is often inserted in the cake. The person who
receives the trinket is declared King or Queen for the day!

Jammin' Jambalaya

Valarie Dennard
Palatka, FL

This recipe has that lively Cajun flavor, but on a milder note so everyone can enjoy it. There are never any leftovers when I serve this dish!

1 lb. boneless, skinless chicken breasts, cut into bite-size pieces
1 lb. andouille sausage, sliced
28-oz. can diced tomatoes
1 onion, chopped
1 green pepper, chopped
1 c. celery, chopped
1 c. chicken broth

2 t. dried oregano
2 t. dried parsley
2 t. Cajun seasoning
1 t. cayenne pepper
1/2 t. dried thyme
1 lb. frozen cooked shrimp, thawed
cooked white rice

Place all ingredients except shrimp and rice in a slow cooker; mix well. Cover and cook on low setting for 7 to 8 hours, or on high setting for 3 to 4 hours. Add shrimp during the last 30 minutes of cooking time. Serve over hot cooked rice. Makes 10 to 12 servings.

No Mardi Gras celebration is complete without some tasty jambalaya...and don't forget to add plenty of colorful beads and a feathered Mardi Gras mask to the table!

Yankee Beef Roast

Rebecca Apple
Grannis, AR

My grandmother often referred to certain foods as "Yankee"
or sometimes "Irish." This dish is my own take on her
Yankee Beef Roast. I serve it over cooked rice.

1/2 t. seasoned salt
3 to 4-lb. beef chuck or
   rump roast
14-1/2 oz. can stewed tomatoes

10-3/4 oz. can cream of
   mushroom soup
1-oz. pkg. onion soup mix

Spray a large slow cooker with non-stick vegetable spray. Sprinkle
seasoned salt in slow cooker; place roast on top. In a microwave-safe
bowl, combine tomatoes with juice and soup. Microwave on high
setting for 3 minutes; stir well and pour over roast. Sprinkle with onion
soup mix. Cover and cook roast on high setting for 5 to 6 hours, until
tender. Serves 8 to 10.

Old-Fashioned Pot Roast

Becky Butler
Keller, TX

This tastes just like the pot roast your grandmother used to make.
Just put it all in the slow cooker and go! This recipe can also be used
for a whole turkey breast...just substitute turkey gravy mix.

2 to 3-lb. beef chuck or
   rump roast
1/2 c. water
1-oz. pkg. ranch salad dressing
   mix

1-oz. pkg. Italian salad dressing
   mix
1.2-oz. pkg. brown gravy mix

Place roast in a slow cooker; add water. Sprinkle dry seasoning mixes
over roast. Cover and cook on low setting for 6 to 7 hours, or on high
setting for 4 to 5 hours. Remove roast to a cutting board; let stand for
15 minutes. Slice roast thinly across the grain. Return sliced beef to
juices in slow cooker. Serves 6 to 8.

Slow-Cooker Barbacoa

Aimee Shugarman
Liberty Township, OH

My husband challenged me to create this spicy dish. Not only did I exceed his expectations, but I also ended up with a recipe that is so easy to prepare in the slow cooker! You can adjust the heat in the dish by increasing or decreasing amount of chipotle peppers you add. We like to serve it with cilantro-lime rice.

3 to 4-lb. beef chuck roast
3 bay leaves
1 c. cider vinegar
juice of 2 limes
3 chipotle peppers in adobo
　　sauce, drained
4 cloves garlic
1 T. ground cumin
1 T. dried oregano

1-1/2 t. salt
1-1/2 t. pepper
1/2 t. ground cloves
1 c. chicken broth
flour tortillas
Toppings: shredded Colby Jack
　　cheese, shredded lettuce,
　　guacamole

Place roast and bay leaves in a large slow cooker. In a food processor or blender, combine vinegar, lime juice, peppers, garlic and seasonings. Process on high until smooth. Pour vinegar mixture and broth over roast. Cover and cook on low setting for 6 to 8 hours, until roast is fork-tender. Shred beef with 2 forks; return to juices in slow cooker. Serve on tortillas with desired toppings. Serves 8.

Bored with tacos? Serve Mexican-style sandwiches for a tasty change! Called tortas, they're hollowed-out crusty bread rolls stuffed with shredded beef or pork and cheese. Serve cold or toast like a panini sandwich...yum!

Hobo Stew

Jessica Minor
Lawrence, KS

*This warm and cozy recipe is a winter favorite in our home.
I start this on Sunday mornings, and it's ready by the time
we come home from church.*

1 lb. ground beef
1-1/2 t. salt, divided
1/2 t. pepper, divided
4 potatoes, peeled and cubed
4 carrots, peeled and cut into
    chunks

1 onion, cut into chunks
1 c. catsup
1 c. water
1 T. vinegar
1/2 t. dried basil

In a bowl, combine beef, one teaspoon salt and 1/4 teaspoon pepper;
mix well. Shape into one-inch balls. In a skillet over medium heat,
brown meatballs on all sides; drain. Place potatoes, carrots and onion
in a slow cooker; top with meatballs. In a small bowl, combine catsup,
water, vinegar, basil and remaining salt and pepper; pour over
meatballs. Cover and cook on high setting for 4 to 5 hours, until
meatballs are cooked through and vegetables are tender. Serves 6.

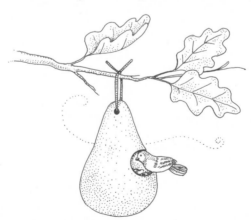

Make gourd bird feeders for feathered friends to enjoy all
winter long. Cut a large opening in a bottle gourd with a craft
knife, then drill a hanging hole in the top and a drainage
hole in the bottom. Fill with a mix of sunflower seeds
and millet to attract a variety of birds.

Warming *Winter* Dishes

Chicken & Wild Rice Soup

Valerie Cliff
Millville, NJ

*I love making this recipe for chilly-weather meals,
and everyone else loves eating it!*

1 lb. boneless, skinless chicken
   breasts or thighs, cubed
1/2 c. onion, chopped
1 c. celery, sliced
1 c. carrot, peeled and diced
6-oz. pkg. long-grain and wild
   rice mix

3 14-1/2 oz. cans chicken broth
2 c. water
1/2 t. pepper
1 T. dried parsley
Optional: 2 t. white vinegar

In a slow cooker, combine all ingredients except vinegar; mix well.
Cover and cook on low setting for 6 to 7 hours, or on high setting for
4 to 5 hours, until chicken is tender. Stir in vinegar, if desired. Sprinkle
with parsley. Serves 9.

Put together a savory soup in your slow cooker, then enjoy
some winter fun with your family. After a snowy hike or
ice skating, a hot, delicious dinner will be waiting
for you...what could be cozier?

Manhattan Clam Chowder

Helen Burns
Raleigh, NC

This zesty soup will help combat the winter doldrums!

1/2 lb. bacon, chopped
1 onion, sliced
2 cloves garlic, minced
28-oz. can whole tomatoes
2 6-1/2 oz. cans minced clams
8-oz. bottle clam juice

1 T. dried thyme
salt and pepper to taste
10-oz. pkg. frozen soup
  vegetables
1 to 2 potatoes, peeled and diced

Add bacon, onion and garlic to a skillet over medium heat; cook and stir until bacon is crisp and onion is tender. Drain; add to a slow cooker. Add remaining ingredients except frozen vegetables and potatoes. Cover and cook on high setting for 2 hours. Add vegetables and potatoes. Cover; reduce heat to low and cook for 3 to 4 hours longer, until vegetables are tender. Serves 4 to 6.

Serve steaming chowder in hollowed-out rounds of sourdough bread. To make yummy croutons, cut the scooped-out bread into one-inch cubes. Season to your liking; lightly toast in an oiled, hot skillet.

Wendi's Veggie-Beef Soup

Wendi Bridwell
Indianapolis, IN

Pair this with some warm bread and sit down to a hearty meal after a busy day! I prep my meat and vegetables the night before. It makes it easy to toss everything together before I dash out the door.

1 lb. beef round steak, cubed
2 c. tomato juice
4 c. water
1/4 c. catsup
3 T. beef bouillon granules
1/4 t. pepper
4 c. potatoes, peeled and diced
2 c. carrots, peeled and diced
2 c. green beans

Combine all ingredients in a slow cooker; stir. Cover and cook on high setting for 7 to 8 hours, adding more water if needed. Makes 8 servings.

If you've strung your Christmas tree with popcorn,
be sure to hang the garlands outside for the birds
to enjoy after the tree comes down!

Mom's Holiday Wings

Vena Oliver
Vienna, IL

My mom always made these wings for holiday gatherings.
They are delicious!

4 to 5 lbs. chicken wings
3 T. oil
1-1/2 c. soy sauce
3/4 c. water

2/3 c. brown sugar, packed
1/2 t. garlic powder
1/4 t. ground ginger

In a large skillet over medium-high heat, brown wings in oil; drain. Transfer to a large slow cooker. In a saucepan, combine remaining ingredients; cook and stir over medium heat until mixture is heated through. Pour over wings. Cover and cook on low setting for 3 to 4 hours, until chicken juices run clear when pierced. Serves 6 to 8.

Upgrade your glass of bubbly!
To one flute of champagne or sparkling white grape juice, add your choice of one tablespoon pomegranate or grapefruit juice, a small scoop of mango sorbet or one teaspoon amaretto liqueur.

Amazing Brie Fondue

Vivian Long
Columbus, OH

I make this rich fondue for all holidays and special events. It disappears quickly...I usually have to make at least a double batch! Spread some on a toasted baguette slice, top with cinnamon, red pepper flakes, herbs and crumbled sausage. It is also great drizzled over fresh and steamed vegetables, or used as a sauce for pasta dishes!

8-oz. brie cheese round,
   rind removed

8-oz. pkg. cream cheese, cubed
1 c. butter, sliced

Cut brie into chunks. Combine all ingredients in a small slow cooker. Cover and cook on low setting for one hour, stirring occasionally, until all ingredients are blended and smooth. Be careful not to let fondue come to a boil. If slow cooker gets too hot, turn it off for about 5 to 8 minutes. Serves 6 to 8.

I plead for memories of olden times, and simple pleasures, and the making of the most delightful music in the world, the laughter of happy children...God bless us all and make us contented. Merry Christmas!

–A.M. Hopkins

Holiday Hot Spiced Tea

Rebecca Apple
Grannis, AR

Our family always looks forward to sharing memories and sipping
our traditional hot tea around the cozy fireplace at Mom's.

4 c. water
2 family-size teabags
1 c. sugar
1 c. brown sugar, packed
1 t. cinnamon
1/2 t. allspice
1/4 t. ground cloves

5 to 6 4-inch cinnamon sticks
1 tart apple, cored and cut into
   large chunks
1 orange, sliced
1 lemon, cut in wedges
1/2 gal. apple juice or
   cranberry-apple juice

In a saucepan over high heat, bring water to a boil; remove from heat.
Steep teabags in hot water for 6 minutes. Remove teabags; add sugars
to saucepan, stirring until dissolved. Add tea and remaining ingredients
to a large slow cooker. Cover and cook on high setting for one to
2 hours, until warmed through. Before serving, strain cinnamon sticks
and fruit. Ladle into mugs; serve warm. Serves 12.

Traditional Mulled Wine

Tiffany Brinkley
Bloomfield, CO

Classic holiday fare!

2 750-ml. bottles dry red wine
1 c. orange juice, or juice of
   3 oranges
1 orange, sliced
3/4 c. sugar

1/4 t. allspice
1/4 t. cinnamon
4 4-inch cinnamon sticks
4 whole cloves

Add all ingredients to a 6-quart slow cooker; stir. Cover and cook on
high setting for 2 hours. Before serving, strain cinnamon sticks and
cloves. Ladle into mugs; serve warm. Serves 8.

Cranberry Meatballs

Lesleigh Robinson
Brownsville, TN

This is a great appetizer for Christmas or anytime.

28-oz. pkg. frozen meatballs
2 3/4-oz. pkgs. brown gravy
   mix
2 14-oz. cans whole-berry
   cranberry sauce

2 T. whipping cream
2 t. Dijon mustard
2 18-oz. bottles barbecue sauce

Place meatballs in a slow cooker. In a bowl, prepare gravy mixes according to package directions; stir in cranberry sauce, cream and mustard. Pour over meatballs; stir. Cover and cook on low setting for 4 to 5 hours, or on high setting for 2 to 3 hours. Before serving, drain gravy mixture; return meatballs to slow cooker to keep warm. Stir in barbeque sauce. Serves 10 to 12.

French Onion Meatballs

Katie Majeske
Denver, PA

Besides being so easy to make, these meatballs are so delicious!

24-oz. pkg. plain or Italian
   frozen meatballs

2 10-1/2 oz. cans French
   onion soup

Spray a slow cooker with non-stick vegetable spray. Add meatballs; pour soup over top. Cover and cook on low setting for 4 hours, or on high setting for 2 hours. Serves 8 to 10.

Don't pass up blue-tinted canning jars that can be filled with rock salt and flickering votive candles...they're perfect for adding color and sparkle to winter windowboxes.

Sticks & Stones

Jewel Sharpe
Raleigh, NC

A delicious and festive party appetizer...there are never
any leftovers at our get-togethers!

14-oz. Kielbasa sausage ring,
   cut into bite-size pieces
32-oz. pkg. frozen mini
   meatballs, thawed

10-oz. jar currant jelly
10-oz. jar red pepper jelly
1 T. Dijon mustard
pretzel sticks or toothpicks

Add sausage and meatballs to a slow cooker. In a microwave-safe
bowl, combine jellies and mustard; microwave on high setting until
mixture is melted and well blended. Pour hot jelly mixture over
kielbasa and meatballs. Cover and cook on low setting for one to
2 hours, until heated through. Serve with pretzel sticks or toothpicks.
Serves 12 to 16.

Pick an evening for a family "card party." Whip up some
special snacks and spend the evening at the kitchen table
signing your Christmas cards. Keep one of your own signed
Christmas cards in a holiday scrapbook...it's a joy to see
the kids' signatures "grow up" over the years.

Crockery Party Mix

Carolyn Deckard
Bedford, IN

We have made this party mix for years to give as gifts for our neighbors, friends, papergirl and mailman. We buy plastic jars that have green or red lids. To add a little color we use strips of Christmas fabric to tie around the lid. Sometimes we add an ornament...cute!

3 c. thin pretzel sticks	1 t. celery salt
2 c. bite-size crispy wheat cereal	1 t. garlic salt
2 c. bite-size crispy rice cereal	1/2 t. salt
2 c. doughnut-shaped oat cereal	2 T. grated Parmesan cheese
2 c. dry-roasted peanuts	1/2 c. butter, melted

In a large bowl, combine pretzels, cereal and peanuts. Sprinkle with seasonings and cheese; drizzle with butter. Toss lightly. Transfer mixture to a large slow cooker. Cover and cook on low setting for 3-1/2 hours. Uncover and cook 30 minutes longer, stirring occasionally. Serve immediately, or store in airtight containers. Serves 10 to 12.

This veggie-packed topiary will certainly "spruce" up your buffet table! Cover a 12-inch styrofoam cone with aluminum foil. Attach broccoli flowerets and cherry tomatoes by sticking one end of a toothpick into the veggie and the other end into the cone. Garnish with cheese "ornaments" cut out with mini cookie cutters...clever!

White Chocolate-Peppermint Clusters

Gladys Kielar
Perrysburg, OH

Homemade candy makes a wonderful holiday gift for family & friends! This tasty concoction is also perfect for shower favors, take-home treats and even bake sales...just scoop into cellophane bags and tie with a festive ribbon.

2 16-oz. pkgs. white melting
    chocolate, chopped
12-oz. pkg. white chocolate
    chips
6-oz. pkg. white baking
    chocolate, chopped

3 T. shortening
16-oz. pkg. pretzel sticks,
    broken into pieces
8-oz. pkg. animal crackers
1 c. peppermint candy, coarsely
    crushed

Combine chocolates and shortening in a 6-quart slow cooker. Cover and cook on low setting for 1-1/2 hours, or until chocolate looks very soft. Stir until smooth. Add pretzels, crackers and peppermint candy; mix well. Drop candy by tablespoons onto wax paper. Let stand one hour, or until firm. Store in an airtight container. Makes 8 dozen.

Set aside leftover candy canes for Valentine's Day decorations! Unwrap and arrange on parchment paper-lined baking sheets. Form pairs into hearts by placing them hook to hook and tail to tail. Bake at 350 degrees for 2 to 4 minutes, until they stick together when the ends are lightly pinched. Let cool, tie with ribbon and hang from windowpanes...so cheery!

Chocolate Peanut Clusters

Christi Assink
South Haven, MI

A tasty and easy recipe for seasonal gift giving!
A cookie scoop makes the job go even faster.

2 16-oz. jars salted dry-roasted
   peanuts
32-oz. pkg. white melting
   chocolate, chopped

4-oz. pkg. sweet baking
   chocolate, chopped
12-oz. pkg. semi-sweet
   chocolate chips

Add all ingredients to a slow cooker. Cover and cook on low setting
for 1-1/2 hours. Turn off slow cooker; let stand 20 minutes and then
mix until blended. Drop by rounded tablespoonfuls onto wax paper.
Let stand one hour, or until firm. Store in an airtight container. Makes
4 dozen.

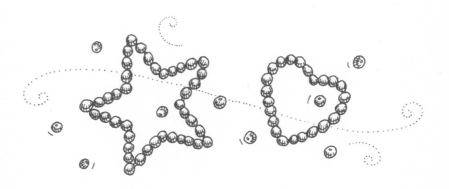

String fresh cranberries onto wire and shape into
a heart for a pretty gift jar tie-on.

Ooey-Gooey Chocolate Cake

Taylor Bielski
Enfield, CT

We have many chocoholics in our family, and everyone loves dessert, so this cake often appears whenever we all get together. During the holidays, we love to serve this warm pudding-like cake topped with seasonal ice cream flavors like mint, pumpkin or gingerbread.

18-1/2 oz. pkg. chocolate
   cake mix
3.9-oz. pkg. instant chocolate
   pudding mix
12-oz. pkg. semi-sweet
   chocolate chips

3/4 c. oil
4 eggs, beaten
16-oz. container sour cream
1 c. water

Spray a slow cooker with non-stick vegetable spray. In a bowl, combine dry cake mix, dry pudding mix and remaining ingredients; stir well. Pour into slow cooker. Cover and cook on low setting for 4 to 5 hours. Scoop into bowls to serve. Serves 8 to 10.

Host a family valentine-making party after dinner's been cleared away. Serve heart-shaped cookies and pink punch, set out plenty of paper crafting supplies, and invite everyone to make handmade cards for their special valentines.

Eggnog Bread Pudding

Hope Comerford
Clinton Township, MI

This bread pudding has the delicious flavor of eggnog and just a hint of the yummy liqueur I soak the raisins in! It isn't too sweet, but just sweet enough. This recipe feeds lots of people, so halve it if you're cooking for a smaller gathering.

2 loaves French bread
1 c. raisins
Optional: 1/2 c. Mexican coffee-
   flavored vodka-based liqueur
8 eggs, beaten
2 t. vanilla extract

1/4 t. ground nutmeg
1/2 t. salt
1/4 c. butter, melted
1 c. sugar
4 c. eggnog
Garnish: whipped cream

The day before preparing bread pudding, cut bread loaves into cubes and spread out to dry. The next day, soak raisins in liqueur, if using, until plump. Meanwhile, mix eggs, vanilla, nutmeg and salt in a very large bowl. Stir in butter, sugar and eggnog. Mix well. Add raisins, with or without liqueur; stir well. Slowly fold in dry bread cubes, stirring until all cubes are coated with egg mixture. Transfer mixture to a large slow cooker that has been sprayed with non-stick vegetable spray. Cover and cook on low setting for 4 to 6 hours, until a knife tip tests clean when inserted into the center. During the last hour of cooking time, place 2 paper towels under the lid to keep the top from getting soggy. Serve warm, topped with whipped cream. Serves 15 to 20.

Dress up dessert plates for a special occasion...before serving, drizzle fruity syrups along the edges or pipe on melted chocolate in fun designs and words.

Gingerbread Pudding Cake

Carrie O'Shea
Marina Del Rey, CA

Delicious, old-fashioned flavor with the modern
convenience of a slow cooker.

1/4 c. butter, softened	1/2 t. cinnamon
1/4 c. sugar	1/2 t. ground ginger
1 egg white	1/4 t. allspice
1 t. vanilla extract	1/8 t. nutmeg
1/2 c. molasses	1/2 c. chopped pecans
1 c. water	6 T. brown sugar, packed
1-1/4 c. all-purpose flour	3/4 c. hot water
3/4 t. baking soda	2/3 c. butter, melted
1/4 t. salt	Garnish: whipped topping

In a large bowl, beat butter and sugar until light and fluffy. Beat in egg white and vanilla. In a separate small bowl, combine molasses and water. In another bowl, combine flour, baking soda, salt and spices. Gradually add flour mixture to butter mixture alternately with molasses mixture, beating well after each addition. Fold in pecans. Pour into a greased 3-quart slow cooker. Sprinkle with brown sugar. Combine hot water and butter; pour over brown sugar. Do not stir. Cover and cook on high setting for 2 to 2-1/2 hours, until a toothpick inserted near the center of cake tests clean. Turn off slow cooker; let stand for 15 minutes. Serve warm, scooped into bowls and garnished with whipped topping. Serves 6 to 8.

Be sure to pick up a pint or two of ice cream in peppermint, cinnamon and other delicious seasonal flavors when they're available. What a special touch for holiday desserts!

Warm Fruited Pudding

Emily Martin
Ontario, Canada

Use your slow cooker to slowly steam this deliciously moist pudding. Displayed on a cake stand, it adds a pretty, festive touch to your holiday buffet!

3/4 c. butter, softened
3/4 c. sugar
2 eggs
1/2 c. orange or apple juice
1 c. all-purpose flour
3/4 t. baking powder
1/2 t. baking soda
1 t. salt
1 t. cinnamon
1/2 t. allspice
1 c. dry bread crumbs
2 c. raisins
1-1/2 c. mixed candied fruit, chopped

In a large bowl, beat butter and sugar until fluffy. Beat in eggs, one at a time; stir in juice. In a separate bowl, combine remaining ingredients; mix well. Gradually add butter mixture to flour mixture; stir until moistened. Pour into a greased 8-cup pudding mold. Cover with greased aluminum foil. Place on a rack in a large slow cooker. Pour boiling water into slow cooker; fill to halfway up the sides of pudding pan. Cover and cook on high setting for 4 hours. Carefully remove pudding mold from slow cooker; invert onto a serving plate. Serves 16.

Make fragrant fire starters from ingredients found around the kitchen! Mix together short cinnamon sticks, dried orange peel and whole cloves. Tuck inside a cardboard tube and wrap the roll with kraft or wrapping paper, securing the ends with twine. Toss several in a gift tote for gift-giving.

Dad's Rice Pudding

Charla Sackmann
Orange City, IA

Creamy rice pudding for dessert, for breakfast or for a snack!
My dad cooked his pudding on the stovetop, but otherwise it's
just the same...a tasty warm treat for those cold winter months.

1 c. long-cooking rice, uncooked
8 c. milk
1 c. sugar
3 eggs, beaten
1/4 c. whipping cream

1/4 t. salt
3/4 t. cinnamon
2 t. vanilla extract
1 c. raisins

Spray a 4-quart slow cooker with non-stick vegetable spray. Pour in rice, milk and sugar. Cover and cook on low setting for 4 hours. In a bowl, combine eggs, cream, salt, cinnamon and vanilla; stir well. From the slow cooker, scoop out 1/2 cup of hot rice mixture and add it to the egg mixture in the bowl. Continue scooping rice mixture, 1/2 cup at a time, and stirring it into egg mixture, until about half of rice mixture has been added. Return contents of bowl to the slow cooker and stir in raisins, mixing well. Cover and cook on high setting for one hour longer, until mixture is thick and creamy and rice is tender. Serves 6 to 8.

Save a few winter snowballs, wrapped in aluminum foil
and stowed in the freezer, for the annual Fourth of July party.
Your guests will be delighted!

Simply Speedy Springtime

Top o' the Morning Irish Oats

Debi Gilpin
Sharpsburg, GA

You can use any combination of dried fruit in this wonderful overnight breakfast...try cranberries, cherries, blueberries and figs.

1 c. Irish steel-cut oats,
  uncooked
1 c. dried fruit, chopped
4 c. water

1/2 c. half-and-half
Garnish: butter, brown sugar,
  cream or milk

Combine all ingredients except garnish in a slow cooker. Cover and cook on low setting for 8 to 9 hours. Stir well before serving. Garnish as desired. Serves 3 to 4.

Perk up morning place settings in a wink...fill pint-size jelly jars with cheery spring blooms.

Shamrock Breakfast Bake

Julianne Saifullah
Lexington, KY

This overnight Southwestern-inspired breakfast bake, studded with green, is a fun way to greet the morning on St. Patrick's Day. This recipe can be doubled for a larger gathering...why not surprise your co-workers? They'll certainly feel lucky!

1/2 lb. ground pork breakfast sausage, browned and crumbled
4-oz. can diced green chiles, drained

1/2 onion, diced
1/2 green pepper, diced
1-1/2 c. shredded Monterey Jack cheese
10 eggs, beaten

Spray a slow cooker with non-stick vegetable spray. Add 1/3 of sausage to slow cooker; top with 1/3 each of chiles, onion, pepper and cheese. Repeat layers, ending with a layer of cheese. Pour eggs over top. Cover and cook on low setting for 7 to 8 hours, until cooked through. Serves 4 to 5.

Make the most of a warm spring morning...take breakfast outdoors! Toss a quilt over the table and serve some warm muffins with homemade jam and fresh fruit.

Tea Room Broccoli-Cheese Soup

Lisa Hardwick
Plainfield, IN

This recipe was inspired by a local tea room that I loved to visit with my family. Their soup was the best I had ever had! Sadly, the tea room closed, but my mother-in-law knew how much I loved the soup and she created this replica for me. It's really yummy, and the recipe means a lot to me because she took the time to make it just for me.

1/2 c. margarine
16-oz. pkg. frozen broccoli cuts
2 10-3/4 oz. cans cream of
　　chicken soup
2 10-3/4 oz. cans cream of
　　mushroom soup

4 c. milk
16-oz. pkg. pasteurized process
　　cheese spread, cubed

In a skillet over medium heat, melt margarine. Add broccoli; cook and stir for 5 to 10 minutes. Add broccoli mixture to a slow cooker; stir in remaining ingredients. Cover and cook on low setting, stirring occasionally, for 3 to 4 hours. Serves 8 to 10.

A well-loved teapot that's been handed down makes
a sweet spring centerpiece...just add fresh-cut
tulips and daffodils from the garden.

French Country Chicken

Teri Lindquist
Gurnee, IL

I am very proud to share my favorite slow-cooker recipe with you! This recipe is completely my own, and we really love it. It has a very fancy taste but takes only minutes to prepare. The wine in this recipe really makes this dish, but broth can be substituted.

1 onion, chopped
6 carrots, peeled and sliced on the diagonal
6 celery stalks, sliced on the diagonal
6 boneless, skinless chicken breasts
1 T. fresh tarragon, chopped
1 T. fresh thyme, chopped

pepper to taste
10-3/4 oz. can cream of chicken soup
1-oz. pkg. onion soup mix
2 T. cornstarch
1/3 c. dry white wine or chicken broth
cooked rice or mashed potatoes

Place onion, carrots and celery in a large slow cooker; arrange chicken on top. Sprinkle with herbs and pepper. In a bowl, combine soup and soup mix; spoon over chicken. Cover and cook on high setting for 4 hours, stirring after one hour. About 10 minutes before serving, whisk cornstarch into wine or broth until smooth. Pour over chicken; stir well. Cook, uncovered, for 10 minutes longer, or until sauce thickens. Serve over rice or mashed potatoes. Serves 6.

Make sure to use the right-size slow cooker...they work best when at least half of the crock is filled.

Brown Sugar-Honey Ham

Hope Comerford
Clinton Township, MI

Baking your ham in the slow cooker is the perfect solution for busy holiday gatherings! You don't have to worry about changing oven temps or trying to squeeze something else in the oven. I've made this recipe with a boneless ham as well as a bone-in spiral-cut ham. Both were awesome!

1 to 1-1/2 c. brown sugar, packed
1/2 t. ground cloves

6-lb. spiral-cut boneless or bone-in cooked ham
2 to 3 T. honey

In a small bowl, combine brown sugar and cloves. Sprinkle about 1/4 cup of brown sugar mixture in a large slow cooker. Place ham in slow cooker, flat-side down. Drizzle honey over top. Pat remaining brown sugar mixture all over ham. Cover and cook on low setting for 4 hours. During the last hour of cooking time, baste ham with melted brown sugar mixture. Serves 10.

Lemon-Lime Ham

Pauletta Dove
Williamson, WV

I've made this easy, crowd-pleasing ham for years...everyone always asks for it! Use your choice of a boneless or semi-boneless ham.

6-lb. cooked ham

20-oz. bottle lemon-lime soda

Place ham in a 5 to 6-quart slow cooker; pour soda over top. Cover and cook on low setting for 8 to 10 hours. Slice to serve. Serves 10.

If you're having trouble fitting your ham into the slow cooker, shave a bit off the side with your knife and lay it on its side. It's the perfect solution!

Creamy Mac & Cheese

Paula Forman
Lancaster, PA

My daughter, now grown, always signed me up to make my slow-cooker macaroni for Girl Scouts, 4-H and many school events. She always came home with an empty crock! For an easy meal, just stir in some cooked shrimp or Kielbasa sausage.

16-oz. pkg. elbow macaroni, uncooked
1/4 c. margarine, sliced
2 c. milk

1 t. salt
8-oz. pkg. pasteurized process cheese spread, cubed
1 c. shredded Cheddar cheese

Cook macaroni according to package directions, until just barely tender; drain. Add macaroni and remaining ingredients to a slow cooker. Cover and cook on low setting for one hour, stirring occasionally. Serves 6 to 8.

It's easy to get more veggies into your family's meals.
Keep frozen vegetable blends on hand to toss into
scrambled eggs, soups or even mac & cheese for
a lunch with a nutritional punch!

Simple Sunday Roast

Pam Massey
Marshall, AR

There's nothing better any night of the week than a hearty beef roast with potatoes and carrots. It's simple, good food that brings back memories of Sunday dinners after church with family.

3 to 4-lb. beef chuck roast
1 T. oil
salt and pepper to taste
5 to 6 potatoes, quartered

1 onion, sliced
16-oz. pkg. baby carrots
2 cubes beef bouillon
1/4 c. hot water

Place roast in a large slow cooker; drizzle with oil and turn to coat. Add salt and pepper to taste. Place vegetables around roast. In a small bowl, dissolve bouillon in hot water. Pour over vegetables in slow cooker. Slowly add more water, until roast is just barely covered. Cover and cook on low setting for 6 to 8 hours, until roast reaches desired doneness. Remove roast and vegetables to a serving platter; slice roast to serve. Serves 8.

Don't forget the gravy! Reserve one to 1-1/2 cups of liquid from the slow cooker. Using one envelope of brown gravy mix, follow the instructions to whip up a delicious stovetop gravy in no time.

Simply Speedy Springtime

Creamy Scalloped Potatoes

Stephanie Carlson
Sioux Falls, SD

Comfort food at its creamiest...these hot and bubbly scalloped potatoes are so easy to make in the slow cooker!

14-1/2 oz. can chicken broth,
   warmed
1/4 c. all-purpose flour
1 c. whipping cream
1 t. salt

1/8 t. pepper
1 onion, diced
6 potatoes, peeled and thinly
   sliced
1 bay leaf

Spray a slow cooker with non-stick vegetable spray. In a bowl, whisk together broth and flour until smooth. Add cream, salt, pepper and onion; stir well. Arrange potato slices in slow cooker; pour broth mixture over top. Add bay leaf. Cover and cook on low setting for 6 to 8 hours, stirring occasionally. Discard bay leaf before serving. Serves 8 to 10.

It's a good idea to test new slow-cooker recipes by staying nearby and checking the dish often...but don't lift the lid! That way, you'll know exactly how long the recipe takes to cook in your slow cooker.

Chicken & Spring Vegetables

Diana Chaney
Olathe, KS

When asparagus is finally in season, I can't wait to add it to all my favorite dishes. This stew is bursting with fresh flavors!

1-1/2 lbs. boneless, skinless chicken thighs, cubed
2 c. baby carrots, halved lengthwise
1 leek, white and light green parts only, sliced
1 T. fresh tarragon, chopped
12-oz. jar chicken gravy

1/3 c. dry white wine or chicken broth
1 T. all-purpose flour
1/2 t. salt
1/2 lb. fresh asparagus, trimmed and cut into 2-inch lengths
1/3 c. frozen peas, thawed

Put chicken, carrots, leek and tarragon in a slow cooker. Pour gravy over top. In a small bowl, whisk together wine or broth, flour and salt. Pour into slow cooker; toss to coat. Cover and cook on low setting for 5 to 8 hours, until chicken and vegetables are tender. Turn to high setting. Add asparagus and peas. Cover and cook on high setting for 10 to 15 minutes, until asparagus is crisp-tender. Serves 6.

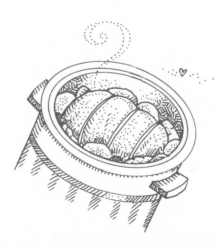

Fresh vegetables like potatoes, carrots and onions should be placed in the bottom and along the sides of a slow cooker, with the meat on top, as they generally take longer to cook.

Split Pea Soup

Krista Marshall
Fort Wayne, IN

Even though I do 99 percent of the cooking in our house, it's nice to know that if for some reason I couldn't, our family wouldn't starve because my husband is a pretty amazing cook. He has a few recipes that are his "signature" dishes, and this is one of them.

2 12-oz. pkgs. dry split peas
1 lb. carrots, peeled and finely
   diced
1 onion, finely diced
1 lb. cooked ham, diced
salt and pepper to taste

Add all ingredients to a slow cooker; add enough water to cover. Cover and cook on high setting for 6 to 8 hours, stirring occasionally, until peas cook down and soup becomes very thick. Add additional water to reach desired consistency, if needed. Serves 8 to 10.

Need to feed a few extra guests? It's easy to stretch a slow cooker full of soup! Some quick add-ins are orzo pasta, ramen noodles, instant rice or canned beans. Add cooked ingredients to slow cooker, and simmer for just a few minutes until heated through.

Lemon-Sage Chicken

Kristen Queen
Stillwater, OK

I love to cook a whole chicken, and with my handy-dandy slow cooker, it's so easy! After you remove the chicken from the slow cooker, keep all those wonderful juices. Once they've cooled, strain and pour into a plastic container. Refrigerate for a few hours and skim fat from the surface. Easy chicken broth!

4 to 5-lb. whole chicken, thawed
  if frozen
dried sage and pepper to taste
1/4 c. butter, sliced

2 cloves garlic, coarsely chopped
1 lemon, sliced
additional dried sage to taste

Pat chicken dry. Place chicken in a large slow cooker, breast-side up. Sprinkle with pepper and sage; place butter and garlic inside the cavity. Sprinkle lemon slices with sage. Very carefully separate the chicken skin from the meat on the breast; slide lemon slices under the skin on each side. Pull legs together; tie with kitchen string. Rub chicken with additional sage. Cover and cook on low setting for 6 to 7 hours, until a meat thermometer inserted into the thickest part of the thigh registers 165 degrees. Carefully remove chicken to a platter. Let stand for 10 to 15 minutes before carving. Serves 4 to 6.

For golden, crispy skin, transfer your slow-cooked chicken to a rimmed baking dish when cooking time is complete. Bake at 500 degrees for 15 minutes. It's okay if your chicken is so moist and tender it falls apart into pieces...it will still be delicious!

Spinach Soufflé

Nancy Wise
Little Rock, AR

Spice up this yummy spinach bake by substituting Mexican pepper cheese and stirring in some red pepper flakes and diced jalapeños!

2 10-oz. pkgs. frozen chopped
   spinach, thawed and drained
2 c. small-curd cottage cheese
1 c. pasteurized process cheese
   spread, cubed

3 eggs, beaten
2 T. butter, diced
1/4 c. all-purpose flour
1/2 t. salt

In a 3-quart slow cooker, combine all ingredients; mix well. Cover and cook on low setting for 2-1/2 hours, or until set and cheese is melted. Serves 8.

Because slow cookers can sometimes dilute the intensity of seasonings over a long period of time, flavorful herbs and spices are best added near the end of cooking.

St. Patrick's Day Corned Beef Dinner

Marilyn Morel
Keene, NH

Enjoy the heavenly aroma that will fill your house. This is sooo good! Serve with warm slices of buttered rye bread.

2 onions, sliced
2 cloves garlic, minced
6 redskin potatoes, halved
3 carrots, peeled and cut into
    chunks
2 bay leaves

1 head cabbage, quartered
3 to 4-lb. corned beef brisket
1 c. water
1/2 c. brown sugar, packed
1 T. mustard
1/2 t. ground cloves

In a large slow cooker, layer onions, garlic, potatoes, carrots, bay leaves and cabbage. Place corned beef on top; add water. Cover and cook on low setting for 10 to 11 hours, or on high setting for 5 to 6 hours. During last hour of cooking, combine brown sugar, mustard and cloves; spread over beef. Cover and cook for one hour longer. Discard bay leaves before serving. Slice corned beef to desired thickness; serve with vegetables. Serves 8 to 10.

If you're making corned beef & cabbage for St. Patrick's Day, add some Irish whimsies to the dining table. Toss gold foil-covered chocolate coins around place settings, add a touch o' green with a shamrock plant centerpiece and play traditional Irish music during dinner.

Simply Speedy Springtime

Slow-Cooker Irish Stew

Amy Shilliday
Tampa, FL

*This traditional slow-cooked Irish stew makes a hearty meal
when served over cooked barley, rice or steel-cut oats.*

1/2 c. all-purpose flour
1 T. salt
1 t. cracked pepper
1 to 2 lbs. stew beef or lamb,
  cubed
2 T. lard or shortening
3 potatoes, peeled and diced

2 carrots, peeled and diced
1-oz. pkg. beefy onion soup mix
2 10-oz. cans beef gravy
1 c. Irish stout or beef broth
additional salt and pepper
  to taste

Combine flour, salt and pepper in a large plastic zipping bag. Add meat;
shake to coat. Place coated meat in a colander and shake over the sink
to remove excess flour. Melt lard or shortening in skillet over medium-
high heat. Brown meat in skillet; drain. Add meat and remaining
ingredients to a slow cooker. Cover and cook on low setting for 6 to
8 hours, or until meat and vegetables are tender. Serves 6 to 8.

Mix up some lucky green popcorn balls for St. Patrick's Day!
Combine one cup corn syrup and 1/2 cup sugar in a saucepan.
Bring to a boil; boil for one minute. Remove from heat and
stir in one small package of lime gelatin mix. Pour mixture
over three to four quarts of popped popcorn in a large
heatproof bowl. Butter your hands and form mixture
into balls. Add a stick, if desired.

Reuben Bake

Dorothy McConnell
Brooklyn, IA

Celebrate St. Patrick's Day with this easy slow-cooker casserole inspired by the classic Reuben deli sandwich!

16-oz. pkg. wide egg noodles, cooked
12-oz. can corned beef, drained and chopped
3-1/2 c. sauerkraut

6 slices American cheese
16-oz. container sour cream
10-3/4 oz. can cream of chicken soup
6 slices Swiss cheese

In a greased 4-quart slow cooker, layer half the noodles; top with half the corned beef. Top with all the sauerkraut and all the American cheese. Stir together sour cream and soup; spoon half of sour cream mixture over American cheese. Layer with remaining noodles, corned beef and sour cream mixture; top with Swiss cheese. Cover and cook on high setting for 2 hours, or until hot and bubbly. Reduce setting to low; cover and cook for one to 2 hours longer. Before serving, stir to combine layers. Serves 6 to 8.

The easiest-ever way to cook egg noodles...bring a big pot of water to a rolling boil, then add the noodles. Remove from heat, cover and let stand for 20 minutes, stirring twice. Perfect!

Loaded Potato Soup

Kitra Ludlow
Bloomington, IN

Everyone asks for the recipe whenever I take
this hearty soup to carry-ins.

32-oz. pkg. frozen hashbrowns
    with onions and peppers,
    thawed
8-oz. pkg cream cheese, diced
10-3/4 oz. can cream of
    mushroom soup
10-3/4 oz. can cream of celery
    soup
10-3/4 oz. can cream of chicken
    soup
1/4 c. onion, minced
salt and pepper to taste
Garnish: shredded Cheddar
    cheese, chopped green
    onions, crumbled bacon

Place hashbrowns in a slow cooker. Add remaining ingredients
except garnish; stir. Cover and cook on high setting for 4 hours.
Garnish individual servings with cheese, green onions and bacon.
Serves 6 to 8.

For a change, spice up Loaded Potato Soup with
crushed tortilla chips, shredded Pepper Jack cheese
and chopped jalapeño peppers!

Luck of the Irish Corned Beef & Cabbage

Pat Beach
Fisherville, KY

My dear friend Jennifer shared this incredible recipe with me many years ago. It's super-easy and also by far the best corned beef & cabbage you will ever eat! Serve with mashed potatoes on the side.

2-1/2 to 3-lb. corned beef brisket
   with seasoning packet
1 head cabbage, cut into large
   wedges

2 12-oz. cans regular or
   non-alcoholic beer

Place corned beef in a large slow cooker, fat-side up. Place cabbage on top. Pour beer over cabbage and beef; sprinkle seasoning packet on top. Cover and cook on high setting for 8 to 10 hours, until beef and cabbage are very tender. Before serving, remove fat from beef; slice and serve with cabbage. Serves 6.

For each petal on the shamrock
this brings a wish your way:
Good health, good luck, and happiness
for today and every day.

–Irish toast

Reuben Dip

Jane Snider
Somerset, OH

I don't always have time to make everyone individual Reuben sandwiches, so I put this in the small slow cooker so people can enjoy it whenever they are ready!

2 2-oz. pkgs. corned beef, chopped
15-oz. can sauerkraut, drained
8-oz. bottle Thousand Island salad dressing

2 6-oz. pkgs. shredded Swiss cheese
shredded wheat or rye crackers

Place all ingredients except crackers in a small slow cooker. Cover and cook on low setting for 2 hours, stirring once or twice, until bubbly and cheese is melted. Serve with crackers. Serves 6.

Celebrate spring by giving a good friend a garden in a can! Fill a vintage watering can with a variety of flower, vegetable and herb seeds...add some gloves, a few garden markers and a gardening magazine.

Asian Pork & Noodles

Sandra Sullivan
Aurora, CO

This is weeknight cooking at its yum-yum best. You'll think you are at the best Asian restaurant!

3 c. low-sodium chicken broth
1/4 c. soy sauce
1/4 c. Chinese rice wine,
    dry sherry or water
3 T. brown sugar, packed
4 cloves garlic, pressed
2-inch piece fresh ginger, peeled
    and sliced
2 pieces star anise
1/2 t. kosher salt

3-lb. boneless pork shoulder
    roast
1 head bok choy, coarsely
    chopped
3-1/2 oz. pkg. rice vermicelli
    noodles or spaghetti,
    uncooked
Garnish: chopped fresh cilantro,
    red pepper flakes

In a large slow cooker, combine chicken broth, soy sauce, rice wine, sherry or water, brown sugar, garlic, ginger, star anise and salt. Add pork; cover and cook on low setting for 8 hours. Shred pork with 2 forks. Add bok choy to slow cooker. Cover and cook about 20 minutes longer. Add noodles to slow cooker, making sure they are fully submerged. Cover and cook for 10 minutes longer, or until tender. Divide pork, bok choy and noodles among 4 bowls and ladle in some of the broth. Sprinkle with cilantro and red pepper flakes. Serves 4 to 6.

Slow cooking keeps moisture inside, causing condensation to form on the lid. To avoid spilling into the crock, always lift the lid straight up, rather than tilting, when stirring or adding ingredients.

Slow-Cooker Lettuce Wraps
Aimee Shugarman
Liberty Township, OH

A perfect dish that can serve as an appetizer or a main dish. And unlike most restaurant varieties, these lettuce wraps are mushroom-free...which makes them kid-friendly at our house!

2 lbs. ground turkey
1 onion, finely chopped
3 stalks celery, finely chopped
3/4 c. hoisin sauce, divided
3/4 c. soy sauce
1/4 c. water
3 cloves garlic, minced
1 T. fresh ginger, peeled
   and grated
2 T. brown sugar, packed

1 T. sesame oil
1 T. hot chili oil
5-oz. can bamboo shoots,
   drained and finely chopped
8-oz. can water chestnuts,
   drained and finely chopped
14-oz. can bean sprouts, drained
1/4 c. fresh cilantro, snipped
12 leaves iceberg lettuce

In a skillet over medium heat, brown turkey with onion; drain. Transfer turkey mixture to a large slow cooker. Add celery, 1/2 cup hoisin sauce, soy sauce, water, garlic, ginger, brown sugar, sesame oil, chili oil, bamboo shoots and water chestnuts. Mix well. Cover and cook on low setting for 6 hours. Before serving, stir in bean sprouts and cilantro. Serve by scooping a generous spoonful onto each lettuce leaf; drizzle with remaining hoisin sauce. Makes 6 servings.

Watch yard sales for vintage glass or china items for decorating your garden. A glass globe perched in a birdbath or mismatched saucers bordering the flowerbed add character!

Thai Peanut Chicken

Patricia Olinik
Quebec, Canada

*I found this recipe one day when I was searching for something
new to try. It has since become one of my staple recipes,
and I always look forward to the next time I get to make it!*

3/4 c. salsa
1/4 c. creamy peanut butter
3/4 c. light coconut milk
2 T. lime juice
1 T. soy sauce
1 t. sugar
2 cloves garlic, finely chopped
2 T. fresh ginger, peeled and
   grated, or 1 T. ground ginger

2 lbs. boneless, skinless chicken
   thighs, each cut into 2 to
   3 pieces
cooked rice
Garnish: chopped peanuts,
   chopped fresh cilantro

Combine salsa, peanut butter, coconut milk, lime juice, soy sauce,
sugar, garlic and ginger in a slow cooker; mix well. Add chicken; stir
to coat. Cover and cook on low setting for 8 hours, or until chicken is
very tender and sauce has thickened. Serve over rice; garnish as
desired. Serves 4.

You can make perfectly steamed, fluffy rice in the slow cooker
too! Rub one tablespoon butter all over the inside of the
slow cooker. Add one cup long-cooking rice, 2 cups water
and salt to taste. Cover and cook on high setting
for 2 to 2-1/2 hours, stirring once or twice.

Chicken Parisienne

Brooke Sottosanti
Brunswick, OH

This easy dish is always a huge hit with my family...
even my picky eater likes it!

6 boneless, skinless chicken
  breasts
salt and pepper to taste
10-3/4 oz. can cream of
  mushroom soup
1/2 c. white wine or chicken
  broth

2 4-1/2 oz. cans sliced
  mushrooms, drained
1 c. sour cream
1/4 c. all-purpose flour
1/4 t. paprika, or to taste
cooked noodles or rice

Place chicken in a slow cooker; sprinkle with salt and pepper. In a
bowl, mix together soup, wine or broth and mushrooms. In a separate
small bowl, combine sour cream and flour. Add sour cream mixture to
soup mixture; mix well. Spoon over chicken; sprinkle with paprika.
Cover and cook on low setting for 6 to 8 hours. Serve over noodles or
rice. Serves 6.

Slow cookers come in so many sizes, you might want to
have more than one! A 4-quart size is handy for recipes that
will feed about four people, while a 5-1/2 to 6-quart one is
just right for larger families and potluck-size recipes.
Just have room for one? Choose an oval slow cooker...
whole chickens and roasts will fit perfectly.

Homey Chicken-Lentil Soup

Chandra Carver
Danielsville, GA

*I created this recipe to use up some leftover rotisserie chicken
and other odds & ends from the pantry. It's super-easy
to modify it to fit your personal tastes!*

1-1/2 c. dried lentils
14-1/2 oz. can fire-roasted
   Tex-Mex style diced tomatoes
14-1/2 oz. can sliced carrots
15-oz. can corn
2 cubes chicken bouillon

1 to 2 T. ground cumin
1 t. red pepper flakes
2 T. dried, minced onion
2 cloves garlic, finely minced
3 to 4-lb. deli roast chicken,
   boned and shredded

Add all ingredients to a slow cooker. Add water to slow cooker until
ingredients are just covered. Cover and cook on low setting for 5 to
6 hours, until lentils are tender. Serves 6.

Plant a portable herb garden! Tuck several herb plants inside
a vintage tin picnic basket...so easy to carry into the kitchen
when it's time to snip fresh herbs. Try easy-to-grow herbs
like parsley, chives, oregano and basil. They'll add
delicious flavor to any meal.

Savory Shrimp Bisque

Sue Denson
Bay Springs, MS

Crawfish and crabmeat make tasty substitutions!

2 10-3/4 oz. cans cream of
  potato soup
10-3/4 oz. can of mushroom
  soup
8-oz. pkg. cream cheese, cubed
15-1/4 oz. can corn, drained

1 to 2 T. Cajun seasoning
1 lb. frozen small shrimp,
  thawed
1 bunch green onions, chopped
1/2 c. margarine
1 qt. half-and-half

Mix soups, cream cheese, corn and seasoning in a slow cooker. Cover and cook on high setting for one to 2 hours, until heated through. In a skillet over medium heat, sauté shrimp and onions in margarine until shrimp are pink. Add shrimp mixture to slow cooker; stir in half-and-half. Cover and cook on low setting for one hour longer. Serves 4 to 6.

When cooking seafood in the slow cooker, add it during the last hour of cooking time, or it may overcook and have a rubbery texture.

Wednesday Salmon Loaf

Robin Hill
Rochester, NY

Weeknights are busy for our family, so I depend on my slow cooker to help keep us out of the drive-thru lane! This easy recipe is one of our favorites. Just add a steamed veggie or tossed salad.

2 15-oz. cans salmon, drained
14-1/2 oz. can diced tomatoes
4 c. dry bread crumbs
1 green pepper, chopped
1 t. lemon juice
10-3/4 oz. can cream of
    onion soup
4 eggs, beaten

1 t. garlic powder
1 t. Greek seasoning
2 chicken bouillon cubes,
    crushed
10-3/4 oz. can cream of celery
    soup
1/4 to 1/2 c. milk

In a bowl, combine salmon, tomatoes with juice and remaining ingredients except cream of celery soup and milk. Mix well. Pour into a slow cooker that has been sprayed with non-stick vegetable spray. Cover and cook on low setting for 4 to 6 hours. Before serving, combine cream of celery soup and milk in a saucepan; cook and stir over medium heat until heated through. Spoon over individual servings. Serves 6.

Try slow-poaching salmon in your slow cooker. Add one cup water and 1/2 cup white wine to a slow cooker; cover and cook on high for 30 minutes. Add salmon fillets, one sliced onion, one sliced lemon, a sprig of fresh dill or 1/2 teaspoon dill weed, and salt and pepper to taste. Reduce heat to low; cover and cook for 20 minutes, or until salmon flakes easily with a fork.

Easy Cheesy Veggies

Amy Hunt
Traphill, NC

Who can resist double-cheesy goodness?

10-3/4 oz. can Cheddar cheese
   soup
2 t. Worcestershire sauce
20-oz. pkg. frozen new potato
   wedges

16-oz. pkg. baby carrots
1/4 c. celery, diced
1-1/4 c. frozen peas
1 c. shredded Cheddar cheese

In a bowl, combine soup and Worcestershire sauce; mix well and set aside. In a 4-quart slow cooker, combine all vegetables except peas; pour soup mixture over top. Cover and cook on low setting for 6 to 7 hours. Before serving, stir in peas and cheese. Cover and cook for 10 minutes longer, or until cheese is melted. Serves 6 to 8.

Hosting a ladies' luncheon? Impress your guests with a yummy slow-cooker brie! Add a round of brie cheese to a slow cooker, and top with 1/3 cup chopped candied pecans and 1/4 cup chopped sweetened dried cranberries. Cover and cook on low setting for 4 hours, or on high setting for 2 hours. Serve with sliced apples, slices of crusty bread or crisp crackers.

Scalloped Potatoes & Ham

Tina George
El Dorado, AR

Using my slow cooker all year 'round lets me focus on doing other things...and supper will still be ready on time! I could make a meal out of this dish alone. But my family wouldn't have that...so, I serve it up with fried okra, sweet corn and homemade dinner rolls.

6 russet potatoes, sliced
   1/4-inch thick
1-1/2 lb. cooked ham steak,
   diced
10-3/4 oz. can cream of
   mushroom soup

1-1/4 c. water
1 c. shredded Cheddar cheese
grill seasoning to taste

Layer potatoes and ham in a slow cooker. In a bowl, combine soup, water, cheese and seasoning. Pour mixture over potatoes and ham. Cover and cook on high setting for 3-1/2 hours, until potatoes are fork-tender. Reduce heat to low. Cover and cook for one hour longer. Serves 4.

Try this easy substitution for canned cream soups. In a bowl, combine one tablespoon softened butter, 3 tablespoons flour, 1/2 cup low-fat milk, 1/2 cup chicken broth and salt and pepper to taste. Use as you would one 10-3/4 ounce can of cream soup.

Penn Dutch Ham Potpie

Nicole Manley
Great Lakes, IL

*When I was in elementary school, our school cafeteria made a version
of this. As I got older I decided it was time to recreate the memory!
You can also substitute turkey or chicken.*

1-lb. cooked ham steak, diced
6 c. water
3 to 4 potatoes, peeled and
    cubed
1 onion, chopped

1/2 c. celery, chopped
1/2 c. carrot, peeled and chopped
1 T. dried parsley
salt and pepper to taste

Add ham and water to a large slow cooker. Cover and cook on low
setting for 5 hours. Add remaining ingredients. Cover and cook on
low setting for 2 hours longer, or until vegetables are tender. About
15 minutes before serving, add Potpie Squares; stir. Cover and cook
for 15 minutes longer, or until squares are fully cooked. Serves 6.

Potpie Squares:

1 egg, beaten
2 to 4 T. water

pepper to taste
1 c. all-purpose flour

In a large bowl, whisk together egg, water and pepper. Add flour, a
little at a time, until a soft dough forms. On a floured surface, roll out
dough 1/4-inch thick. With a sharp knife, cut into 2-inch squares.

Perk up a package of brown
& serve dinner rolls! Before
baking, brush tops with a little
beaten egg and sprinkle with
shredded Parmesan cheese
and Italian seasoning.

Roasted Potatoes

Krista Marshall
Fort Wayne, IN

*I love making these for holidays, parties or family gatherings.
A great side to any meal that cooks while I'm spending time
with guests instead of in the kitchen.*

6 potatoes, cut into wedges
1/4 c. water
1 t. salt
1 t. pepper
1 t. garlic powder

1 t. dried, minced onion
1 t. Italian seasoning
1 t. dried parsley
1/2 t. dill weed
1/4 c. butter, diced

Place potatoes in a slow cooker. Sprinkle with water and seasonings.
Stir to combine. Dot with butter. Cover and cook on low setting for
5 to 6 hours, until tender. Serves 4 to 6.

Make no-fuss hard-boiled eggs in your slow cooker! Cover
six eggs with water in the slow cooker, cover and cook on
low for 3-1/2 hours. They'll be perfectly hard-boiled for
use in egg salad sandwiches, tossed salad toppings and
deviled eggs...or to dye for the Easter Bunny to hide!

Teriyaki Pork Roast

Lori Jodoin
Novi, MI

My all-time favorite slow-cooker recipe is for this delicious teriyaki-inspired pork roast. It never lets me down!

3/4 c. apple juice
2 T. sugar
2 T. soy sauce
1 T. vinegar
1 t. ground ginger

1/4 t. garlic powder
3 lb. boneless pork loin
2-1/2 T. cornstarch
3 T. cold water

Combine all ingredients except pork, cornstarch and water in a lightly greased slow cooker. Add pork loin; turn to coat and place fat-side up. Cover and cook on low setting for 7 to 8 hours. Remove pork loin and keep it warm. In a large saucepan, combine cornstarch and cold water; stir until smooth. Stir in all the juices from roast. Bring to a boil over high heat. Cook and stir for 2 minutes, or until gravy thickens. Slice pork loin; serve with gravy. Serves 6.

A simply "tweet" Easter treat...marshmallow chick s'mores! Arrange graham crackers on a baking sheet; top each with a square of chocolate and a marshmallow chick. Place under a broiler just until marshmallows begin to soften. Remove from oven and top with another graham cracker. Yum!

Sweet-and-Sour Chicken

Patricia Wissler
Harrisburg, PA

*This yummy meal travels well. I often take it to
new moms and recovering shut-ins.*

2 lbs. boneless, skinless chicken
   breasts or thighs, cubed
2 12-oz. jars sweet-and-sour
   sauce

16-oz. pkg. frozen stir-fry
   vegetable blend, thawed
cooked rice

Combine chicken and sauce in a slow cooker. Cover and cook on low
setting for 8 to 10 hours, until chicken is tender. About 10 minutes
before serving, stir in vegetables. Cover and cook on high setting for
10 minutes, or until vegetables are crisp-tender. Serve over rice.
Serves 6.

'Twas Easter Sunday.
The full-blossomed trees
Filled all the air with fragrance and with joy.

–Henry Wadsworth Longfellow

Chicken with Potatoes & Spinach

Susan Styles
Mishawaka, IN

My children never liked plain cooked spinach, but they gobble up this yummy chicken dish almost as fast as I can serve it! We've enjoyed this recipe for years and it never fails to fill tummies.

3 boneless, skinless chicken
  breasts
salt and pepper to taste
1 c. onion, chopped
1 lb. new Yukon Gold or
  redskin potatoes, quartered

8-oz. pkg. fresh baby spinach
10-3/4 oz. can cream of celery
  soup, divided

Arrange chicken on a baking sheet lined with aluminum foil. Broil for 3 to 4 minutes on each side, or until very lightly golden. Cut chicken into one-inch cubes; season with salt and pepper. Layer onion, potatoes and spinach in a slow cooker. Add half the soup. Add chicken; top with remaining soup. Cover and cook on high setting for 3 to 4 hours, or on low setting for 6 to 8 hours, stirring once or twice. Serves 6.

Fresh, green salads are the perfect go-along to hearty
slow-cooked dinners. Keep it oh-so easy by picking up
a bag of fresh spinach and tossing with toasted pecans
and dried cranberries or apricots. Top with a splash
of balsamic vinegar dressing...mmm!

Chicken Lasagna Florentine

Nicole Draves
Pembroke, MA

My family just loves this creamy and different lasagna.

10-oz. pkg. frozen chopped
    spinach, thawed and drained
2 c. cooked chicken, diced
2 10-3/4 oz. cans cream of
    chicken soup
8-oz. container sour cream
1 c. milk
1/2 c. shredded Parmesan
    cheese

1/3 c. onion, chopped
1/2 t. salt
1/4 t. pepper
1/8 t. nutmeg
9 lasagna noodles, uncooked
1 c. shredded mozzarella cheese

In a large bowl, combine all ingredients except lasagna noodles and mozzarella cheese; stir well. Spray a 5-quart slow cooker with non-stick vegetable spray. Place 3 lasagna noodles in slow cooker, breaking noodles in half to fit. Spread 1/3 of spinach mixture over noodles; sprinkle with 1/3 cup mozzarella cheese. Repeat layers, ending with mozzarella cheese. Cover and cook on high setting for one hour. Reduce heat to low. Cover and cook on low setting for 5 hours longer, or until noodles are tender. Serves 8.

Hosting a Mothers' Day brunch or an afternoon tea? Dress up the table by tying pretty scarves around chair backs, then tuck a tulip in each knot.

Simply Speedy Springtime

Feta Greek Chicken

Beth Bennett
Stratham, NH

I didn't know what to make for dinner, but I had some chicken
in the freezer and I love Greek seasoning...so this is what
I came up with. It turned out surprisingly good!

8 to 10 boneless, skinless
   chicken breasts
2 T. Greek seasoning
1 c. water
1-1/2 c. crumbled feta cheese

2 14-1/2 oz. cans diced
   tomatoes with basil, garlic
   and oregano

Place chicken in a slow cooker; sprinkle with seasoning. In a bowl,
combine water, cheese and tomatoes with juice. Pour over chicken.
Cover and cook on high setting for 3 to 4 hours, until chicken is no
longer pink. Serves 8 to 10.

Chicken Cordon Bleu

Linda Harmon
Garner, NC

If you love traditional Chicken Cordon Bleu, give this easy
slow-cooker version a try! Chicken, ham and Swiss cheese
slow-simmered for hours in a creamy sauce...mmm.

10-3/4 oz. can cream of chicken
   soup
1 c. milk
4 to 6 boneless, skinless chicken
   breasts

1/4 lb. sliced deli ham
1/4 lb. sliced Swiss cheese

In a bowl, combine soup and milk. Pour enough of soup mixture into
a slow cooker to cover the bottom; arrange chicken over top. Cover
chicken with slices of ham and cheese. Pour remaining soup mixture
over cheese. Cover and cook on low setting for 4 to 6 hours, or on
high setting for 2 to 3 hours, until chicken is done. Serves 4 to 6.

Savory Turkey Loaf

Teri Eklund
Olympia, WA

My famous alternative to traditional meatloaf!

2 lbs. ground turkey
3/4 c. dry bread crumbs
1/2 c. applesauce
1 t. poultry seasoning
2 cloves garlic, minced

1/4 c. onion, minced
1 egg, lightly beaten
salt and pepper to taste
1/4 t. paprika

In a large bowl, combine all ingredients except paprika. Mix well. Form into a loaf or a round shape; place in a slow cooker. Sprinkle with paprika. Cover and cook on low setting for 5 to 6 hours. Serves 8.

Crockery Tuna Bake

Shannon Reents
Loudonville, OH

Another of my dear friend Grace's recipes...we adored sharing recipes. She sure had the love for cooking!

3 5-oz. cans tuna, drained
1/2 c. celery, chopped
1/4 c. green pepper, chopped
2 eggs, beaten

1/2 c. milk
1/2 t. salt
1 c. old-fashioned oats,
   uncooked

In a bowl, combine all ingredients; mix well. Press mixture into a 9"x5" loaf pan; set pan inside a large oval slow cooker. Cover and cook on high setting for one to 2 hours. Remove pan from slow cooker; set on a wire rack to cool. Slice to serve. Serves 6 to 8.

Pick up some paper plates, cups and napkins in seasonal designs. They'll make dinner fun when time is short, plus clean-up will be a breeze.

Simply Speedy Springtime

Tasty Green Beans

Stephanie Edgington
West Milton, OH

Our family loves this easy-to-make side...it doesn't require precious oven or stovetop space during big family gatherings!

1/2 lb. bacon
4 14-1/2 oz. cans cut green
   beans, drained

2 14-oz. cans chicken broth
1 onion, cut into wedges
salt and pepper

In a skillet over medium heat, cook bacon until crisp. Drain, reserving 1/2 of drippings. Crumble bacon. Add bacon, reserved drippings and remaining ingredients to a slow cooker; stir. Cover and cook on low setting for 7 to 8 hours, or on high setting for 5 hours. Serves 6 to 8.

Chunky Applesauce

Lisa Ann Panzino DiNunzio
Vineland, NJ

There's nothing like homemade applesauce, and it can't get any easier than this yummy slow-cooker version!

10 to 12 apples, peeled, cored
   and cut into large chunks
1/2 c. water

3/4 c. sugar
Optional: 1 t. cinnamon

Combine all ingredients in a slow cooker. Cover and cook on low setting for 8 to 10 hours, until apples break apart easily. Mash apples. Serve warm, or refrigerate in an airtight container. Serves 4 to 6.

Some recipes only call for half an onion, so save prep time on a future recipe... just chop and freeze the other half right away.

Mexican Roast Pork Stew

Joanne Callahan
Far Hills, NJ

I like experimenting with low-fat recipes, and this one is a real crowd-pleaser! Served over brown rice, it makes an excellent and nutritious one-dish meal.

4 to 6-lb. pork picnic roast,
    cut into bite-size pieces
1/4 c. chili powder
2 T. ground cumin
1 T. coriander
1 sweet onion, chopped
2 cloves garlic, pressed
1 T. oil

2 28-oz. cans stewed tomatoes
15-oz. can black beans, drained
    and rinsed
2 dried poblano peppers, finely
    chopped and seeds removed
2 c. apple juice or water
cooked brown rice

Toss pork with seasonings. In a skillet over medium heat, sauté pork, onion and garlic in oil until browned on all sides. To a large slow cooker, add pork mixture, tomatoes with juice, beans, peppers and juice or water. Cover and cook on low setting for 9 hours. Serve ladled over rice. Serves 10 to 12.

Use thrift-store flatware to create clever garden markers.
Slide a empty seed packet between the tines of a fork,
or slip over an old spoon or knife.

Southwest Meatloaf

Sharon Murray
Lexington Park, MD

Are you a meatloaf fan? This recipe includes salsa for a Southwest flair, so you can make it as spicy as you want! Try a mellow tomato salsa, or for a kick, a hot cilantro and garlic green sauce.

2 lbs. ground beef
1 c. onion, chopped
1/4 t. salt
1/4 t. pepper

3 slices bread, torn
1 egg, beaten
1/2 c. catsup
1/2 c. chunky salsa

Spray a slow cooker with non-stick vegetable spray. Combine all ingredients except catsup and salsa; shape mixture into a loaf. Place in slow cooker. Make a shallow indention in the top of the meatloaf. In a small bowl, combine catsup and salsa; pour over meatloaf. Serves 6 to 8.

If you'd like to remove your meatloaf from the slow cooker before serving it, here's a tip for creating an aluminum foil "sling." Tear off two lengths of foil long enough to fit in bottom of slow cooker and extend 3 inches over each side. Fold each foil strip lengthwise to form 2-inch wide strips. Arrange foil strips in criss-cross fashion in the slow cooker, pressing strips in the bottom and extending ends over sides. When the meatloaf is finished cooking, just lift the overhanging "handles" to remove the meatloaf!

Porcupine Meatballs

JoAnn

*Tender, rice-filled meatballs in a tasty, tomatoey sauce...
it's an oldie but a goodie!*

1-1/2 lbs. ground beef
1/2 c. dry bread crumbs
1/4 c. onion, minced
2 T. green pepper, chopped
1 c. long-cooking rice, uncooked
1-1/2 t. salt

1/2 t. pepper
1 egg, slightly beaten
10 3/4-oz. can tomato soup
1 c. water
1 T. Worcestershire sauce

In a large bowl, combine beef, bread crumbs, onion, green pepper, rice, salt, pepper and egg; mix well. Shape beef mixture into 24 meatballs, about 1-1/2 inches in diameter. Place meatballs in a slow cooker. In a separate bowl, combine soup, water and Worcestershire sauce. Pour over meatballs. Cover and cook on low setting for 7 to 8 hours, or on high setting for 4 to 5 hours. Makes 4 to 6 servings.

Long-cooking rice is best for slow-cooker recipes...it stays firm, while instant rice can overcook and become mushy.

Family-Favorite Swiss Steak

Kris Couveau
Soldotna, AK

I've been making this tender steak in yummy tomato gravy for more than 30 years. It's so delicious served with fluffy mashed potatoes!

1 c. all-purpose flour
salt and pepper to taste
2 lbs. beef round steak, cut into
   serving-size pieces
2 T. oil
1 onion, diced

1 c. celery, diced
1 green pepper, diced
10-1/2 oz. can tomato soup
1/4 c. water
1 T. cornstarch
mashed potatoes

In a large plastic zipping bag, combine flour, salt and pepper. Add steak pieces, turning and pressing to coat well in flour mixture. In a skillet over medium-high heat, heat oil; brown steaks on both sides, but do not cook through. To a slow cooker, add onion, celery, green pepper and soup. Whisk together water and cornstarch; pour over top. Add steak pieces. Cover and cook on high setting for 6 to 8 hours, or on low setting for 10 to 12 hours. Stir before serving. Serve steak over mashed potatoes; top with tomato gravy from slow cooker. Serves 5 to 6.

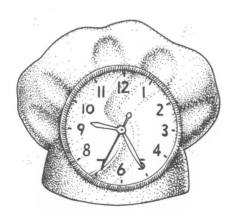

Long, slow cooking is ideal for inexpensive cuts of meat because it provides plenty of time for tenderizing. Easy on the budget!

"Rotisserie" Chicken

*Sara Tatham
Plymouth, NH*

This is a simple, delicious way to prepare chicken. It really does taste a lot like the rotisserie ones you can buy at the deli. You will have falling-off-the-bone, beautifully seasoned meat, plus a lot of good broth that you can freeze for later! I've also used bone-in chicken breasts instead of a whole chicken, with good results.

3 to 4-lb. whole roasting
   chicken

Montreal seasoning or lemon-
pepper seasoning to taste

Pat chicken dry and place it in a large slow cooker. Sprinkle generously with seasoning. Cover and cook on low setting for 8 to 10 hours, or on high setting for 4 to 5 hours. Serves 4 to 6.

Don't toss the bones from a roast chicken! Turn them
into delicious broth...it's oh-so-simple with a slow cooker.
Combine bones with a big handful of chopped onion, carrot
and celery. Add 6 cups water. Cover and cook on low setting
for 8 to 10 hours. Strain, refrigerate and skim fat, then
freeze in one-cup portions. They'll be ready to use in
your favorite recipes.

Cheesy Corn for a Crowd

*Jennifer Stacy
Hamler, OH*

*I make this yummy corn casserole every time my family gets together.
My nieces & nephews can't get enough!*

4 15-1/4 oz. cans corn, drained
4 15-oz. cans creamed corn
8-oz. pkg. shredded Cheddar
  cheese
8-oz. pkg. shredded mozzarella
  cheese

2 8-1/2 oz. pkgs. corn muffin
  mix
16-oz. container French onion
  dip
4 eggs, beaten

Combine all ingredients in a large bowl. Prepare a 6-quart slow cooker
by either spraying with non-stick vegetable spray or putting in a
disposable liner. Pour mixture into slow cooker. Cover and cook
on high setting for 4-1/2 hours, or on low setting for 9 hours.
Serves 15 to 18.

You can even bake bread in your slow cooker! Rub butter
generously over a 9"x5" loaf pan and a frozen bread loaf. Set
the pan in an oval slow cooker and add the loaf. Cover and
cook on low setting until the dough thaws and begins to rise,
about 2 to 3 hours. Turn to high setting and continue
cooking for another 2 to 3 hours, until the loaf is golden
and sounds hollow when tapped.

Chicken & Dumplings

Wendy Lickteig
Cresco, IA

My boss and I trade recipes often, and this one
was a huge hit at my home!

4 boneless skinless chicken
  breasts, cubed
2 10-3/4 oz. cans cream of
  chicken soup
1/4 c. onion, finely chopped

2 c. water
1 cube chicken bouillon
2 10-oz. tubes refrigerated
  biscuits

Combine all ingredients except biscuits in a slow cooker. Cover and
cook on low setting for 5 to 6 hours. About 30 minutes before serving,
tear biscuit dough into one-inch pieces. Add to slow cooker, stirring
gently. Increase setting to high. Cover and cook on high setting for
30 minutes longer, or until biscuits are fluffy and cooked through.
Serves 4.

Tender baked potatoes from your slow cooker...it's easy! Pierce
6 baking potatoes with a fork and wrap each in aluminum
foil. Stack in a slow cooker. Cover and cook on low setting
8 to 10 hours, or on high setting for 2-1/2 to 4 hours.

Simply Speedy Springtime

Pork & Rice in Tomato Sauce

Connie Wagner
Manchester, PA

My husband and my father both really love this meal.

30-oz. can tomato sauce
15-oz. can stewed
   tomatoes
1-3/4 to 2 c. water

1-1/2 c. long-cooking rice,
   uncooked
4 pork chops
salt and pepper to taste

Combine tomato sauce, stewed tomatoes with juice, water and rice in a slow cooker; mix well. Sprinkle chops with salt and pepper; add to slow cooker, pressing them down into the liquid. If they are not covered, add more water. Cover and cook on low setting for 6 to 8 hours, adding more water if needed. Serves 4.

Papaya-Tomato Chicken

Rowena Sjovall
Lithia, FL

A very simple and flavorful slow-cooker recipe using papaya jelly and zesty canned tomatoes.

4 chicken leg quarters
salt and pepper to taste
1 c. papaya jelly

10-oz. can diced tomatoes
   with green chiles

Pat chicken dry; sprinkle with salt and pepper. Place in a slow cooker. In a bowl, combine jelly and tomatoes with juice. Pour over chicken. Cover and cook on low setting for 6 hours. Serves 4.

If there's too much liquid in the slow cooker at the end of cooking time, spoon the excess liquid into a small saucepan. In a small bowl, blend one tablespoon of cooking liquid and 2 teaspoons cornstarch. Whisk back into saucepan. Bring mixture to a boil; reduce heat and simmer until thickened. Stir into the slow cooker before serving.

The Preacher's Mushroom Steak
Sherry Nagel
Brook, IN

The old joke that everyone fed the preacher chicken when he came to visit prompted my mother to make this steak using our own farm-raised beef. Serve with mashed potatoes or rice, a chopped garden salad and warm dinner rolls.

1-1/2 lbs. beef round steak, cut
    into serving-size pieces
1 T. oil
10-3/4 oz. can cream of
    mushroom soup

4-oz. can mushroom stems and
    pieces, drained
2 c. water
1 t. seasoned salt
1/2 t. pepper

In a skillet over medium-high heat, brown steak on both sides in oil. Place steak in slow cooker; add remaining ingredients in the order given. Cover and cook on high setting for 6 to 8 hours, or on low setting for 9 to 10 hours. Serves 4 to 6.

When spring cleaning time rolls around, slow-cooker dishes make mealtime a breeze. Add all the ingredients, turn it on and forget about it. Now, throw open the windows and air out the quilts with no worries about what's for dinner!

Simply Speedy Springtime

Orange & Ginger Beef Ribs

Lee Beedle
Church View, VA

I always thought beef ribs and marmalade would go together perfectly in the slow cooker. When I tried this recipe, I knew right away it was a keeper...even my picky son raved about it! I sometimes toss in chunks of onions and peppers for variety.

1/3 c. soy sauce
3 T. brown sugar, packed
3 T. white vinegar
2 cloves garlic, minced
1/2 t. chili powder

1 T. fresh ginger, peeled
  and minced
3 lbs. boneless beef short ribs
1/3 c. orange marmalade

In a large plastic zipping bag, combine all ingredients except ribs and marmalade. Add ribs to bag; turn to coat well. Refrigerate at least 2 hours to overnight. Drain ribs, reserving marinade. Place ribs in a large slow cooker. Add marmalade to reserved marinade; mix well and pour over ribs. Cover and cook on high setting for 4 hours, or on low setting for 6 to 8 hours. Serves 6.

To thicken a slow-cooker recipe, remove the lid and cook on high setting for the final 30 minutes of cooking time.

Lemon Poppy Seed Upside-Down Cake

Rogene Rogers
Bemidji, MN

This cake makes its own custard-like topping...mmm!

15.6-oz. pkg. lemon poppy seed
   quick bread mix
1 egg, beaten
8-oz. container light sour cream

1-1/4 c. water, divided
1 T. butter
1/2 c. sugar
juice of 1 lemon

In a bowl, mix dry bread mix, egg, sour cream and 1/2 cup water until well moistened. Spread batter in a lightly greased 3-1/2 quart slow cooker. Combine remaining water and other ingredients in a saucepan; bring to a boil. Pour boiling mixture over batter; do not stir. Cover and cook on high setting for 2 to 2-1/2 hours, until edges are lightly golden. Turn off slow cooker; let stand for about 30 minutes with lid slightly ajar. When stoneware is cool enough to handle, invert cake onto a serving plate. Serves 10 to 12.

A garden party is the perfect occasion for swapping seeds and cuttings. Treat your guests to a pair of new garden gloves, and share a little potted cutting as a party favor.

Cherry Delight

Kathy Grashoff
Fort Wayne, IN

This scrumptious warm dessert is delicious topped with vanilla ice cream or whipped cream. You can also use apple or blueberry pie filling instead of cherry!

21-oz. can cherry pie filling   1/2 c. butter, melted
18-1/4 oz. pkg. yellow cake mix   1/3 c. chopped walnuts

Place pie filling in a slow cooker. In a bowl, combine dry cake mix and butter. Mixture will be crumbly. Sprinkle over filling; top with walnuts. Cover and cook on low setting for 2 to 3 hours. Serves 10 to 12.

For easy, no-dye decorated Easter eggs, just attach double-sided adhesive dots to hard-boiled eggs and roll in glitter. So cute!

Bananas Foster

Audrey Lett
Newark, DE

Go bananas with this fun new way to make a classic dessert!

4 bananas, sliced
1/4 c. butter, melted
1 c. brown sugar, packed
1/4 c. rum or 2 t. rum extract
1 t. vanilla extract

1/2 t. cinnamon
1/4 c. chopped walnuts
1/4 c. sweetened flaked coconut
vanilla ice cream

Layer sliced bananas in a slow cooker. Combine butter, brown sugar, rum or rum extract, vanilla and cinnamon in a small bowl; sprinkle over bananas. Cover and cook on low setting for 2 hours. About 30 minutes before serving, top bananas with walnuts and coconut. Cover and cook on low setting for 30 minutes longer. Serve over scoops of vanilla ice cream. Serves 4.

Keep your blooms standing tall in a floral centerpiece.
Just slip stems into clear drinking straws and they'll
keep their heads up all day!

Chocolate Mocha Bread Pudding
Kay Marone
Des Moines, IA

It's the perfect dessert if you love coffee or chocolate...or both!

1 loaf hearty white bread, cubed	1 c. sugar
4 c. milk	1 c. brown sugar, packed
1/4 c. whipping cream	1/4 c. baking cocoa
6 eggs, beaten	1 T. instant espresso powder
1 T. vanilla extract	1 c. semi-sweet chocolate chips

Spray a large slow cooker with non-stick vegetable spray. Place bread cubes in slow cooker. In a bowl, whisk together milk, cream, eggs and vanilla. In a separate bowl, combine sugars, cocoa and espresso powder; add to milk mixture, stirring well. Pour milk mixture over bread cubes. Stir and press bread cubes into milk mixture until they are fully coated. Sprinkle with chocolate chips. Cover and cook on high setting for 2 to 3 hours, or until set. Serves 8 to 10.

What could be more perfect for a tea party than tea roses?
Float blossoms in shallow glass bowls filled with water,
or arrange them in single-color or mixed bouquets
all around the house.

Coconut-Mango Rice Pudding

Vickie

A delectably different dessert for your springtime gathering.

1 c. long-cooking white rice,
    uncooked
1-1/2 t. cinnamon
4 slices fresh ginger, peeled
    and diced
15-oz. can coconut milk

4 c. milk
1 c. sugar
2 t. vanilla extract
2 T. sesame seed
1 mango, peeled and diced
honey to taste

Place rice, cinnamon and ginger in a slow cooker. In a bowl, whisk together milks, sugar and vanilla. Pour over rice. Cover and cook on high setting for 3 to 3 -1/2 hours, stirring once or twice, until rice is fully cooked and milk is absorbed. Just before serving, toast sesame seed in a dry skillet over medium heat until just golden. Serve individual portions of rice pudding topped with diced mango, honey and sesame seed. Makes 8 to 10 servings.

The world's favorite season
is the spring.
All things seem possible
in May.

–Edwin Way Teale

Slow & Easy
Summer

Down-On-the-Farm Breakfast Cobbler

Bev Westfall
Berlin, NY

This easy apple dish is wonderful! Cook it overnight while you sleep or after you wake up in the morning. Either way, it's delicious and so convenient to make.

8 tart apples, peeled, cored
   and sliced
2 c. granola
1/4 c. butter, melted

1/4 c. sugar
1 T. cinnamon
juice of 1 lemon

Combine all ingredients in a lightly greased slow cooker; mix well. Cover and cook on low setting for 7 to 9 hours, or on high setting for 2 to 3 hours. Serves 6 to 8.

Summer breeze so softly blowing
In my garden pinks are growing,
If you'll go and send the showers,
You may come and smell my flowers.

–Vintage children's book

Slow & Easy Summer

Slow-Cooked Stone Fruit

Jean Tonkin
Sydney, Australia

This is such a practical way of using beautiful summer stone fruit when there is a lot of it around. It doesn't matter if it's marked or slightly damaged. If using dark-skinned peaches and plums, the fruit will turn a dark rich crimson color. Delicious!

2 lbs. peaches, plums, nectarines
   or apricots
4-inch cinnamon stick

1/2 c. orange or apple juice
Garnish: Greek yogurt or
   whipping cream

Cut fruit in half; remove pits. Do not peel. Lay fruit skin-side down in a single layer in a large slow cooker. It's fine to have a few pieces of fruit in a second layer. Push cinnamon stick into the fruit. Add juice (more juice will be created during the cooking). Cover and cook on low setting for 6 to 8 hours. Remove cinnamon stick before serving. Serve topped with yogurt or cream. Serves 4 to 6.

Very Berry Sauce

Ann McMaster
Portland, OR

Got bushels of berries? Cook up some of this yummy topping. Use it to top pancakes, yogurt, ice cream...or whatever you like!

6 c. fresh or frozen strawberries,
   blueberries or blackberries
1/2 c. sugar

2 T. quick-cooking tapioca,
   uncooked

Combine all ingredients in a slow cooker. Cover and cook on low setting for 4 hours, or on high setting for 2 hours, stirring occasionally. Makes 8 to 10 servings.

Need to peel peaches, pears or tomatoes in a hurry? Simply drop them into boiling water, then submerge them in cold water...the skins will slip right off.

Hot Diggity Dogs

Lynn Mabe
Norwood, NC

My mom makes these saucy dogs for her grandchildren.

16-oz. pkg. hot dogs
3/4 c. catsup
Worcestershire sauce to taste

1/4 c. barbecue sauce
1/2 c. brown sugar, packed
10 hot dog buns

Cut hot dogs into thirds. Place all ingredients into a small slow cooker; stir. Cover and cook on low setting for 4 hours. Serve on buns; top with some sauce from the slow cooker. Serves 6 to 8.

A quick & easy summertime treat...layer blueberries,
strawberry preserves and vanilla ice cream in a parfait
glass. Top with whipped cream and a cherry.
Perfect for the Fourth of July!

Sweet-and-Sour Kielbasa

Doreen Bolduc
Chaplin, CT

*Great for get-togethers! This recipe can easily
be tripled, but use just one cup of catsup.*

1 onion, diced
2 T. butter
14-oz. Kielbasa sausage ring,
   cut into serving-size pieces

1/2 c. brown sugar, packed
1 T. mustard
Worcestershire sauce to taste
1/2 c. catsup

In a small skillet over medium heat, sauté onion in butter. Transfer to a slow cooker; add remaining ingredients. Cover and cook on low setting for 6 hours. Serves 4 to 6.

Daddy's Favorite Dinner

Sara Voges
Washington, IN

*This is one of our summertime favorites, when the just-picked
green beans turn up at the farmers' market!*

14-oz. smoked turkey sausage
   ring, cut into serving-size
   pieces
1/2 onion, cut into chunks
10 new redskin potatoes

2 lbs. fresh green beans,
   trimmed and snapped
salt and pepper to taste
1 to 2 T. olive oil
Optional: 2 T. butter, sliced

Place all ingredients in a slow cooker; stir well. Cover and cook on high setting for 5 hours, or on low setting for 8 to 10 hours. Serves 4 to 6.

Fresh Green Beans & Potatoes

Kathy Grashoff
Fort Wayne, IN

*Such a yummy way to use up your garden's crop
of beans...a perfect summer supper!*

6 to 8 new redskin potatoes
2 lbs. fresh green beans,
    trimmed and snapped
1/4 lb. smoked bacon or cooked
    ham, chopped, or 1 smoked
    ham hock

2 onions, chopped
2 c. water
2 t. salt

Add potatoes and beans to a slow cooker; top with ham or bacon. Spread onions over top. Add water and salt. Cover and cook on low setting for 8 to 9 hours, until beans are tender. Serves 6.

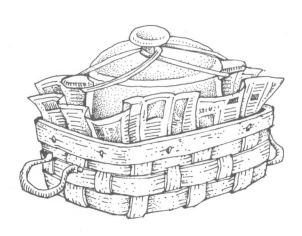

When toting a slow-cooker dish to a potluck, wrap a
rubber band around one handle, bring it up over the lid
and secure it over the other handle...the lid
stays on nice and tight!

Caramelized Onions

Jill Ball
Highland, UT

I love caramelized onions! They are a great topping for anything off the grill...hamburgers, steak or chicken. Making them in the slow cooker is sooo easy.

8 onions, thickly sliced
1/4 c. butter
1/4 c. olive oil

1/2 T. sugar
salt to taste

Add all ingredients to a slow cooker; stir to combine. Cook, uncovered, on low setting for 6 to 8 hours, stirring and scraping sides of crock often. Makes 12 servings.

Hot Dog Topping

Tina Hockensmith
Canton, OH

This tasty topping is a "must" at our cookouts!

1 lb. ground beef, browned and
    drained
32-oz. pkg. refrigerated
    sauerkraut, drained

2 c. tomato juice
1/2 c. brown sugar, packed
salt and pepper to taste

Add all ingredients to a slow cooker; stir well. Cover and cook on low to medium setting for 2 hours, or until heated through. Serves 6 to 8.

Serve up summer salad dressings in Mason jars with a vintage serving spoon...a pretty country touch for any table.

BBQ Beef Sandwiches

Karol Cloutier
Alberta, Canada

A great meal for a day when it's just too hot to cook.

2-1/2 to 3-lb. lean beef chuck
   roast or round steak
1-1/2 c. catsup
1/4 c. brown sugar, packed
1/4 c. wine vinegar
2 T. spicy or Dijon mustard
1 T. Worcestershire sauce

1 t. smoke-flavored cooking
   sauce
1/2 t. salt
1/4 t. pepper
1/2 t. garlic powder
12 sandwich buns, toasted

Place beef in a slow cooker. In a bowl, combine remaining ingredients except buns; pour over beef. Cover and cook on low setting for 8 to 10 hours. Shred beef with 2 forks; stir well. Spoon beef mixture onto toasted sandwich buns; top with additional sauce from slow cooker, if desired. Makes 12 servings.

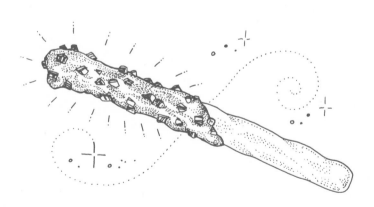

For an easy themed party treat, dip pretzel rods
in melted semi-sweet or white chocolate and
roll them in multicolored sprinkles.

Debbie's Sloppy Joes

Debbie Kraus
Indian Harbor Beach, FL

This easy recipe is perfect for feeding a hungry crowd!

4 lbs. ground beef
1 c. yellow onion, chopped
1 c. green pepper, chopped
2 10-3/4 oz. cans tomato soup
15-oz. can tomato sauce
8-oz. can tomato sauce
3/4 c. brown sugar, packed

1/4 c. catsup
3 T. Worcestershire sauce
1 T. mustard
1 T. dry mustard
1 t. chili powder
1 t. garlic salt
24 sandwich buns, split

In a large skillet over medium heat, brown beef with onion and green pepper; drain. Add beef mixture to a large slow cooker. Add remaining ingredients except buns; stir well. Cover and cook on low setting for 6 to 8 hours, stirring occasionally. Serve on buns. Makes 24 servings.

A quick go-with for a slow-cooker meal...toss steamed green beans, broccoli or zucchini with a little olive oil and chopped fresh herbs.

Chris's Chuckwagon Beans

Christina Mendoza
Alamogordo, NM

I combined three or four of my favorite recipes to create this one.
We always serve these meaty beans with a side of hot cornbread.

1 lb. dried navy or pinto beans,
   rinsed
1 lb. ground beef
1 onion, chopped
1 clove garlic, minced
1 green pepper, chopped

6 c. water
salt to taste
1/2 t. dried oregano
1/4 t. cayenne pepper, or to taste
8-oz. can tomato sauce

Add beans to a large kettle; cover with water. Bring to boiling; boil, covered, for 2 minutes. Remove from heat and let stand for one hour. Drain. Add beans to a large slow cooker. In a skillet, brown beef with onion, garlic and green pepper. Drain. Add beef mixture to beans in slow cooker; stir in 6 cups water and remaining ingredients. Add more water, if necessary, so that bean mixture is covered. Cover and cook on low setting for 10 hours, or on high setting for 6 hours, until beans are tender. Serves 6 to 8.

Serve up Chuckwagon Beans cowboy-style. Spoon stew into enamelware bowls, add a side of cornbread and keep bandannas on hand for fun lap-size napkins.

Warm 3-Bean Salad

Svea Miller
Poultney, VT

*This is an old Pennsylvania Dutch recipe that my mother
often made for family gatherings.*

16-oz. can kidney beans,
   drained
15-oz. can cannellini beans,
   drained
14-1/2 oz. can cut green beans,
   drained
14-1/2 oz. can diced tomatoes,
   drained

15-1/4 oz. can corn, drained
1 t. pickling spice, finely ground
1/4 t. mustard seed
1/2 c. white onion, diced
1/2 c. white vinegar
1-1/2 c. water
hot pepper sauce to taste

Combine all ingredients in a slow cooker; stir well. Cover and cook on
low setting for 4 to 6 hours. Add more water if needed. Serve warm.
Serves 4 to 6.

Safety first! Keep hot foods hot, cold foods cold,
and don't let any picnic foods sit out longer than
2 hours, even if the food looks just fine.

Vegetable Chili

Michelle Taggart
Parker, CO

*I created this recipe one day when I was trying to make chili
healthier for my family. It's chock-full of veggies!*

1 lb. ground beef, browned
   and drained
2 14-1/2 oz. cans diced
   tomatoes
1 onion, diced
2 zucchini, diced
3 carrots, peeled and diced
2 15-oz. cans black-eyed peas,
   drained and rinsed

15-oz. can pinto beans, drained
   and rinsed
15-1/4 oz. can corn, drained
1-1/4 oz. pkg. chili seasoning
   mix
Garnish: shredded Cheddar
   cheese

Add beef, tomatoes with juice and remaining ingredients except
cheese to a slow cooker; mix well. Cover and cook on low setting for
3 to 4 hours. To serve, ladle into bowls and sprinkle with cheese.
Serves 8 to 10.

There's no such thing as too much chili! Top hot dogs and
baked potatoes with extra chili...spoon into flour tortillas
and sprinkle with shredded cheese for quick burritos.

Poblano Corn Chowder

Joshua Logan
Victoria, TX

You'll love this kicked-up corn chowder...a great way to use the hot peppers that seem to multiply overnight in your backyard garden!

4 c. chicken broth
1 T. sugar
2 14-1/2 oz. cans creamed corn
2 c. potato, peeled and diced
2 to 3 poblano chiles, diced and
    seeds removed
10-oz. pkg. frozen corn, thawed

1 lb. boneless, skinless chicken
    breasts or thighs, cubed
1/2 lb. chorizo pork sausage,
    diced
1 c. whipping cream
1/4 c. fresh cilantro, chopped

In a 6-quart slow cooker, combine all ingredients except cream and cilantro. Cover and cook on low setting for 7 to 8 hours, until chicken is cooked through. Before serving, stir in cream and cilantro; warm through. Serves 8.

To enhance the flavor of Poblano Corn Chowder, roast the chiles and thawed corn before adding to the slow cooker. Place chiles and corn in a single layer in a roasting pan. Drizzle with one tablespoon olive oil; toss to coat. Bake at 375 degrees for 30 minutes.

Steak Diane

Jennie Gist
Gooseberry Patch

*If it's too hot to grill outside, you can still enjoy
a great steak...from your slow cooker!*

1 lb. beef tenderloin, sliced
   1/4-inch thick
2 T. butter
1 c. sliced mushrooms
1/2 c. beef broth

1 t. fresh chives, chopped
1 t. fresh parsley, minced
1 t. salt
1/4 t. pepper
Optional: 2 t. brandy

In a skillet over medium-high heat, brown beef in butter for
one minute on each side. Place in a slow cooker. Add remaining
ingredients except brandy. Cover and cook on low setting for 6 to
8 hours, or on high setting for 4 to 5 hours. During the last 30 minutes
of cooking, stir in brandy, if using. Serves 4.

The easiest-ever iced tea! Fill up a 2-quart pitcher with water
and drop in 6 to 8 teabags. Refrigerate overnight. Discard
teabags and add ice cubes and sugar to taste.

Summer Vegetable Fettuccine

Vickie

*Try this meatless pasta dish and discover a new favorite
way to use up your summertime abundance of
zucchini and yellow squash.*

2 T. butter
1 zucchini, sliced
1 yellow squash, sliced
2 carrots, peeled and thinly
   sliced
1-1/2 c. sliced mushrooms
1 lb. broccoli, chopped
4 green onions, sliced
2 to 3 cloves garlic, minced

1/2 t. dried basil
1/4 t. salt
1/2 t. pepper
1 c. grated Parmesan cheese
12-oz. pkg. fettucine pasta,
   uncooked
1 c. shredded mozzarella cheese
1 c. whipping cream
2 egg yolks, beaten

Use butter to grease the inside of a slow cooker. Place vegetables,
seasonings and Parmesan cheese in slow cooker. Cover and cook on
high setting for 2 hours, or until vegetables are tender. Cook pasta
according to package directions; drain. Add pasta, mozzarella cheese,
cream and egg yolks to slow cooker. Stir to blend well. Cover and
cook on high setting for 30 minutes longer, or until heated through.
Serves 6.

A properly working slow cooker uses about
as much electricity as a light bulb, making it more
economical...and cooler...than using the stove!

Creamy Cheesy Corn

Lynda Valley
Decorah, IA

*My family always looks for this yummy, cheesy corn
at our annual family reunions.*

3 16-oz. pkgs. frozen corn
8-oz. pkg. cream cheese, cubed
5 slices American cheese,
   chopped

3 T. butter, sliced
3 T. milk
3 T. sugar

Spray a slow cooker with non-stick vegetable spray. Add all ingredients; stir to mix. Cover and cook on low setting for 4 hours, or until cheese is melted and corn is heated through. Stir once after cheese melts. Serves 10 to 12.

Oh-so clever! Alongside each slow cooker, use wooden
alphabet tiles to spell out recipe names. Guests
will know just what's inside, and it's a fun twist
on the traditional table tent.

Pineapple Baked Beans

Katie Cooper
Chubbuck, ID

This is my mother's recipe...it makes the most
scrumptious baked beans.

28-oz. can baked beans
14-oz. bottle catsup
1-1/2 c. brown sugar, packed
15-1/4 oz. pineapple chunks,
   drained

1/2 lb. bacon, chopped
2 T. Worcestershire sauce
1 T. soy sauce

Add all ingredients to a slow cooker; stir well. Cover and cook on low
setting for 3 to 5 hours. Serves 10 to 15.

Baked Beans with Sausage

Kerry Fountain
Ionia, MI

This is a quick & easy hearty baked bean dish!

1 lb. ground pork sausage,
   browned and drained
48-oz. jar Great Northern beans,
   drained

1 c. brown sugar, packed
1 onion, chopped

Combine all ingredients in a slow cooker. Cover and cook on low
setting for 4 to 6 hours. Serves 4 to 6.

Look for old wooden boxes
with partitions...they were
often used to hold beverage
bottles separately. They
make great containers
for herb gardens or
a sampling of annuals.

Bacon Cheeseburger Dip

Amy Hunt
Traphill, NC

All the tastes of a great cheeseburger in one tasty dip!

6-oz. pkg. real bacon bits,
  divided
1/2 lb. lean ground beef or
  turkey
8-oz. pkg. cream cheese, cubed
2 c. shredded Cheddar cheese

10-oz. can diced tomatoes with
  green chiles
1 t. dried parsley
assorted dippers, such as mini
  bagel chips, tortilla chips and
  sliced green and red peppers

Reserve 2 tablespoons bacon bits; set aside. In a large skillet over medium heat, brown beef or turkey; drain. Reduce heat to low and stir in cheeses, tomatoes with juice and remaining bacon bits. Cook and stir until heated through. Pour mixture into a 2-quart slow cooker. Cover and cook on low setting for 2 to 3 hours. Before serving, stir in parsley and sprinkle with remaining bacon bits. Serve with assorted dippers. Serves 10 to 12.

Slow cookers make family reunion dinners so easy!
While dinner cooks, families can enjoy a game of baseball,
croquet or hide & seek, or just sit in the shade
catching up with one another.

Hot Crab Rangoon Dip

*Karen Schmidt
Racine, WI*

*This is so easy to mix up for a party, and it always
brings loads of compliments.*

2 8-oz. pkgs. cream cheese,
  softened
2 6-oz. cans crabmeat, drained
  and flaked
10-3/4 oz. can cream of shrimp
  soup

1 T. green onion, finely chopped
1 t. lemon juice
2 t. soy sauce
1 t. Worcestershire sauce
rice crackers

Combine all ingredients except crackers in a 3 to 4-quart slow cooker;
mix well. Cover and cook on low setting for 2 to 3 hours. Serve with
crackers. Serves 10 to 12.

Watching fireworks at a friend's house this year? Tote along
a stoneware crock full of this warm, tasty dip. Surround it
with red cherry tomatoes and snowy white cauliflower
flowerets. Add some slices of crunchy carrot, zucchini and
radish cut into star shapes with mini cookie cutters.

Hearty Carrot Soup

Kimberly Ascroft
Merritt Island, FL

When left with a late-season garden full of carrots, I make carrot soup! It's a great way to use 'em up...everybody loves it.

32-oz. container sodium-free
   beef broth
2-1/2 lbs. carrots, peeled and
   sliced
1/4 c. onion, diced

2 cloves garlic, minced
2 T. brown sugar, packed
1 T. ground ginger
1/4 c. whipping cream

In a slow cooker, combine broth, carrots, onion and garlic. Cover and cook on high setting for 5 hours, or on low setting for 8 hours, until carrots break apart easily. Working in batches, transfer contents of slow cooker to a blender or food processor, or use an immersion blender. Blend soup for about one minute, or until desired consistency is reached. Stir in remaining ingredients. Serve warm. Serves 6.

Old-fashioned Mason jars make lovely lanterns for backyard gatherings! Nestle a tea light inside and hang with wire from tree branches or fenceposts. Look for citronella candles to keep mosquitoes away.

Papa's Favorite Cheesy Corn Soup

Kristina Hodgdon
Marco Island, FL

My dad loves this hearty soup, so I named it after him!

1 c. green pepper, chopped
1 c. onion, chopped
6 cloves garlic, minced
1/4 c. butter
2 8-oz. pkgs. cream cheese, cubed
2 c. milk
2 cubes chicken bouillon
2 c. boiling water
2 8-oz. cans corn, drained

2 8-oz. cans creamed corn
6 baking potatoes, peeled and cubed
1 t. salt
pepper to taste
Optional: 1 lb. white fish, such as haddock or tilapia, or other seafood such as clams, crab, shrimp or scallops
Garnish: oyster crackers

In a skillet, sauté green pepper, onion and garlic in butter. Add cream cheese and milk. Cook and stir until cream cheese melts. Add to a slow cooker. Dissolve bouillon in boiling water. Stir into slow cooker. Add remaining ingredients except seafood, if using, and garnish. Cover and cook on high setting for 2 to 3 hours. If using, seafood may be added during the last hour of cooking time. Garnish with crackers.
Serves 10 to 12.

Crusty bread is a must-have alongside hearty soups.
Heat an oven-safe stoneware bowl and tuck slices
inside to keep them toasty at the table.

Zucchini Parmesan

Muriel Vlahakis
Sarasota, FL

Everyone in our family loves my eggplant Parmesan. I thought
I would try this alternative for one summer family gathering,
because we all love Italian food. It was a big hit!

10 zucchini, thinly sliced
2 T. oil
garlic powder to taste
26-oz. jar spaghetti sauce

8-oz. pkg. shredded mozzarella
  cheese
1 to 1-1/2 c. shredded Parmesan
  cheese

Heat oil in a skillet over medium heat. Working in batches, sauté
zucchini until tender. Layer 1/4 of zucchini in a slow cooker; sprinkle
with garlic powder. Spoon 1/4 of sauce over top; sprinkle with 1/4 of
cheeses. Repeat layers 3 times, ending with cheeses. Cover and cook
on low setting for 2 to 4 hours, until cheese melts. Serves 10 to 12.

Make your favorite slow-cooker recipe healthier
by sneaking in a few more chopped veggies!
Adjust seasonings to taste.

Veggie-Stuffed Burritos

Jen Licon-Conner
Gooseberry Patch

It's easy to get the kids to eat their veggies when you
serve these healthy veggie burritos with all the trimmings!

2 T. chili powder
2 t. dried oregano
1-1/2 t. ground cumin
1 sweet or russet potato, peeled
    and diced
15-oz. can black beans or pinto
    beans, drained and rinsed
4 cloves garlic, minced
1 onion, halved and thinly sliced
1 jalapeño pepper, seeded
    and chopped

1 green pepper, chopped
1 c. corn
3 T. lime juice
1 T. fresh cilantro, chopped
8-oz. pkg. shredded Cheddar
    Jack cheese
8 to 10 flour tortillas
Garnish: sour cream

Combine spices in a small bowl; set aside. In a slow cooker, layer potato, beans, half of spice mixture, garlic, onion, peppers, remaining spice mixture and corn. Cover and cook on low setting for 5 hours, or until potato is tender. Stir in lime juice and cilantro. To assemble burritos, spoon some cheese into the center of each tortilla. Top with one cup of veggie mixture from the slow cooker. Wrap and place burritos seam-side down on an ungreased baking sheet. Cover with aluminum foil; bake at 350 degrees for 20 minutes. Serve topped with sour cream. Serves 8 to 10.

Have an overabundance of tomatoes, zucchini or peppers in your garden? Set veggies out in bushel baskets at an end-of-summer party along with paper sacks...invite guests to fill the sacks and take 'em home as party favors!

Stuffed Green Peppers

Ann Presley
Science Hill, KY

On busy days, I can whip up this easy dinner in no time!

6 green peppers, tops and
   seeds removed
salt to taste
1 lb. ground beef chuck
1/2 c. onion, chopped

1/3 c. long-cooking rice,
   uncooked
1/2 t. salt
1-1/4 c. water, divided
1-1/4 c. catsup, divided

Sprinkle insides of peppers with salt; set aside. In a bowl, combine uncooked beef, onion, uncooked rice, salt, 2/3 cup water and 1/4 cup catsup. Mix well. Fill green peppers 2/3 full with beef mixture. Arrange stuffed peppers in a slow cooker, stacking peppers if needed. Combine remaining water and catsup; drizzle over peppers. Cover and cook on low setting for 6 to 8 hours, or on high setting for 3 hours. Makes 6 servings.

Green peppers are so versatile...stuff them with shrimp, ground beef and rice, ham & cheese or Italian sausage.

Cabbage Patch

Jennifer Crisp
Abingdon, IL

Old-fashioned comfort food at its best, and this recipe feeds
a crowd! Leftovers, if you have any, freeze wonderfully.

1-1/2 lbs. ground beef
1 onion, diced
2 14-1/2 oz. cans diced
   tomatoes
2 15-oz. cans kidney beans,
   drained and rinsed
2 14-oz. cans beef broth
3 stalks celery, diced

3 potatoes, peeled and diced
4 carrots, peeled and diced
1 head cabbage, chopped
1 T. sugar
ground cumin, garlic powder,
   pepper and onion salt
   to taste

In a skillet over medium heat, brown beef and onion; drain. Add beef
mixture to a slow cooker; add tomatoes with juice and remaining
ingredients. Mix well. Cover and cook on low setting for 4 to 5 hours,
until vegetables are soft. Serves 10.

If I had my way, I'd remove January from the calendar
altogether and have an extra July instead.

–Roald Dahl

Slow-Cooker Chicken Fajitas

Karen Campbell
Canton, IL

Serve with a side of black beans & rice and corn chips
for a flavorful south-of-the-border feast!

3 green, yellow or red peppers,
   sliced
2 onions, sliced
2 T. garlic, finely minced
8 boneless, skinless chicken
   breasts, cut into thin strips
2 1-1/4 oz. pkgs. taco
   seasoning mix

1 t. coarse salt, divided
1/2 c. olive oil
8 to 12 flour tortillas
Toppings: salsa, guacamole,
   sour cream, shredded Colby
   Jack cheese, chopped black
   olives, diced tomatoes,
   shredded lettuce

Layer half each of peppers, onions, garlic and chicken in a slow cooker; sprinkle with one package taco seasoning and 1/2 teaspoon salt. Repeat layering; drizzle with oil. Cover and cook on low setting for 4 to 6 hours, until chicken is fully cooked and juices run clear. Stir to combine. To serve, spoon chicken mixture onto tortillas, adding desired toppings. Serves 4 to 6.

Summer's bounty of delicious red and yellow peppers can be preserved for winter enjoyment. Fill ice cube trays with diced peppers and water, then freeze. Toss frozen cubes right into simmering dishes for a burst of flavor and color.

Lemon Garlic Chicken

Kimberly Marlatt
Yuma, AZ

This dish is so versatile, super-easy to make and pleasing to even the pickiest of palates. For a side, you can cook up some stir-fry veggies with a bit of the sauce and serve everything over hot rice...yummy!

6 to 8 boneless, skinless chicken
    thighs
2/3 c. soy sauce
1/3 c. lemon or lime juice
2 T. Worcestershire sauce
2 t. rice wine vinegar

1-1/2 t. garlic powder
1 t. sugar
1/2 t. pepper
1/2 t. dry mustard
Optional: 1 to 2 T. cornstarch,
    1 to 2 T. cold water

Spray a 6-quart slow cooker with non-stick vegetable spray; add chicken. In a bowl, combine remaining ingredients except cornstarch and water. Pour over chicken; stir. Cover and cook on high setting for one hour. Reduce heat to low; cook for 3 to 4 hours. To thicken sauce, combine cornstarch and water; stir into slow cooker. Cover and cook for 10 minutes longer, or until sauce thickens. Serves 6 to 8.

Orange Chicken

Rachel Rice
Danville, IL

This simple chicken satisfies our craving for Chinese food without having to call for take-out!

4 boneless, skinless chicken
    breasts
2 12-oz. cans regular or diet
    orange soda

1/2 c. soy sauce
cooked rice

Place chicken in a slow cooker. Pour orange soda and soy sauce over top. Cover and cook on low setting for 4 to 5 hours. Serve over rice. Serves 4.

Savory Low-Country Shrimp & Cheese Grits

Sharon Candler
Charleston, SC

Serve this classic low-country favorite with some warm,
crusty bread and a fresh spinach salad.

6 c. chicken broth
3/4 t. salt
1-1/2 c. long-cooking grits,
  uncooked
1 green pepper, chopped
1/2 red pepper, chopped
6 green onions, chopped
2 cloves garlic, minced
1-1/2 lb. uncooked small
  shrimp, peeled

2 T. butter
1-1/2 c. shredded sharp Cheddar
  cheese
1-1/2 c. shredded Monterey Jack
  cheese
2 10-oz. cans diced tomatoes
  with green chiles, drained
1/4 t. cayenne pepper, or to taste

Combine broth, salt and grits in a slow cooker; stir well. Cover and cook on low setting for 8 to 10 hours. About 2 hours before serving, in a skillet over medium heat, sauté peppers, onions, garlic and shrimp in butter until shrimp turn pink. Add pepper mixture to slow cooker along with cheeses, tomatoes and cayenne pepper. Stir well. Cover and cook on high setting for 2 hours longer. Serves 6 to 8.

Fill your summertime picnic table with whimsies...watch
tealights sparkle in Mason jars filled with sea glass
and serve fruit or tossed salads in new sand pails.

Bayou Gumbo

Sue Neely
Greenville, IL

A warm summer night is the perfect setting for enjoying this
mouthwatering gumbo from deep in the heart of swamp country.

3 T. oil
3 T. all-purpose flour
14-1/2 oz. can diced tomatoes
1/2 lb. smoked pork sausage,
    cut into 1/2-inch slices
2 c. frozen cut okra
1 onion, chopped

1 green pepper, chopped
3 cloves garlic, minced
1/4 t. cayenne pepper
12-oz. pkg. frozen cooked
    medium shrimp, thawed
cooked rice

In a small saucepan over medium heat, combine oil and flour. Cook,
stirring constantly, for 5 minutes. Reduce heat; cook, stirring
constantly, about 10 minutes longer, or until mixture turns reddish-
brown. Place flour mixture in a 3-1/2 to 4-quart slow cooker. Stir in
tomatoes with juice and remaining ingredients except shrimp and rice.
Cover and cook on low setting for 7 to 9 hours. Add shrimp to slow
cooker; mix well. Cover and cook on low setting for 20 minutes longer,
or until heated through. Serve gumbo ladled over rice. Serves 6.

Liven up summer beverages by
adding frozen slices of lemon
or lime. Use them instead of an
ice cube to chill your drink...
no more watered-down drinks,
plus enjoy a refreshing hint
of citrus! To make, just lay
lemon or lime slices flat
on a tray and freeze.

Chicken-Zucchini Parmesan

Brenda Delucia
Poland, NY

This recipe has been a family favorite ever since I created it on a day when the garden was overflowing with fresh vegetables. It is very easy to prepare in the slow cooker.

2 boneless skinless chicken
    breasts, cubed
1 red pepper, chopped
1 green pepper, chopped
1 onion, chopped
2 zucchini, diced
2 yellow squash, diced
1 T. Italian seasoning

1 t. salt
1/2 t. pepper
2 c. spaghetti sauce
2 T. oil
1/4 c. shredded Parmesan
    cheese
1 c. shredded mozzarella cheese

Add all ingredients except cheeses to a slow cooker; mix well. Cover and cook on low setting for 6 to 8 hours. Add cheeses; turn off slow cooker. Serve when cheese is melted. Serves 6 to 8.

Keep camping meals easy with one-skillet and one-pot recipes. Don't forget to pack a slow cooker in the RV too...dinner will practically cook itself!

Easy Cabbage Rolls

Beth Griffith
Orient, OH

*It really doesn't take very long to assemble these cabbage rolls...
comfort food just like Mom used to make!*

1 lb. ground beef chuck
1/2 c. instant rice, uncooked
1 onion, chopped
1 t. salt

1/4 t. pepper
1/4 t. garlic salt
48-oz. can tomato juice, divided
1 head cabbage

In a bowl, combine uncooked beef, uncooked rice, onion, seasonings
and one cup tomato juice; mix well. Pour 1/2 cup remaining tomato
juice into a slow cooker; spread to cover bottom. To assemble rolls,
tear off one cabbage leaf; place a large spoonful of beef mixture on top.
Roll up leaf; place it in the slow cooker, seam-side down. Repeat until
all beef mixture is used. Pour remaining tomato juice over rolls. Cover
and cook on high setting for 6 hours, or until cooked through.
Serves 4 to 6.

Light and fizzy...the perfect drink for brunch! Combine
one cup sugar, 6 cups chilled pineapple juice and
one cup lime juice. Stir in 2 liters sparkling water
and serve over crushed ice.

Crockery Chicken Tagine

Grace Smith
British Columbia, Canada

This Moroccan-inspired stew features richly spiced chicken and squash...give it a try using your fresh-picked tomatoes!

1 butternut squash, peeled and
   cut into 2-inch cubes
2 tomatoes, coarsely chopped
1 onion, chopped
2 cloves garlic, pressed
15-oz. can garbanzo beans,
   drained and rinsed
1 c. chicken broth
1/3 c. raisins

2 t. coriander
2 t. ground cumin
1/2 t. cinnamon
1/2 t. salt
1/4 t. pepper
3 lbs. skinless chicken thighs
10-oz. pkg. couscous, uncooked
1/2 c. green olives

In a large slow cooker, combine squash, tomatoes, onion, garlic, beans, broth and raisins. In a small bowl, combine spices, salt and pepper. Rub spice mixture over chicken; place chicken on top of vegetable mixture. Cover and cook on low setting for 8 hours, or on high setting for 4 hours. About 10 minutes before serving, prepare couscous according to package directions. Stir olives into chicken mixture. Serve chicken mixture ladled over couscous. Serves 6.

For fresh-from-the-garden tasting tomatoes,
always store them at room temperature.

Garden Chicken Pasta

Sharon Metzger
Lititz, PA

One summer, a friend gave me some squash, and I decided to try something different. Now my youngest daughter always requests this recipe when she comes home from college.

3 boneless, skinless chicken
   breasts
16-oz. bottle Italian salad
   dressing
12-oz. pkg. tri-color rotini pasta,
   uncooked

2 zucchini, sliced
2 yellow squash, sliced
Garnish: grated Parmesan
   cheese, sliced black olives

Place chicken in a slow cooker; pour salad dressing over top. Cover and cook on low setting for 6 to 8 hours. About 15 minutes before serving, cook pasta according to package directions; drain. Meanwhile, in a skillet over medium heat, sauté squash using some of the liquid from the slow cooker until tender. Remove chicken from slow cooker; cut into cubes. Add pasta to a large serving bowl; top with chicken and squash. Toss before serving, adding more liquid from the slow cooker, if needed. Garnish with Parmesan cheese and olives. Serves 6.

The ceramic insert in a slow cooker may crack if exposed to abrupt temperature shifts. Don't set a hot crock directly on a cold counter; always put a tea towel down first. Likewise, don't put a crock straight from the refrigerator into a preheated base.

Chile Verde

Kathryn Harris
Valley Center, KS

My family loves Mexican food, and I've long searched for a recipe to duplicate our beloved chile verde at home. I think the flavor of this recipe comes very close, and since it cooks in the slow cooker, it's really easy to make!

3 to 5-lb. boneless pork roast
14-1/2 oz. can stewed or fire-
   roasted diced tomatoes
28-oz. can crushed tomatoes
22-oz. can tomato sauce
5 4-oz. cans diced green chiles
2 c. onion, chopped
1-1/2 T. jalapeño pepper, seeded
   and diced
1/2 c. fresh cilantro or parsley,
   chopped

2 T. ground cumin
1 T. garlic powder
1 T. sugar
1/4 t. ground cloves
1/4 t. salt
1/4 c. lemon juice
4 c. hot water
20 to 24 corn or flour tortillas
Garnish: guacamole, sour cream,
   queso fresco, tortilla chips

To a large slow cooker, add pork, tomatoes with juice and remaining ingredients except tortillas and garnish. Cover and cook on high setting for 4 hours, or on low setting for 6 hours. Before serving, shred pork with 2 forks; stir into mixture in slow cooker. Skim off fat, if needed. Fill tortillas with pork mixture; add toppings as desired. Serves 10 to 12.

If you love super-spicy chili, give New Mexico chili powder a try. Sold at Hispanic and specialty food stores, it contains pure ground red chili peppers, unlike regular chili powder which is a blend of chili, garlic and other seasonings.

Chicken Cacciatore

Helen Burns
Raleigh, NC

*This simple recipe is one of my favorite ways to use
the best of the summer's ripe red tomatoes.*

1 onion, sliced
3 cloves garlic, sliced
1 T. butter
4 boneless, skinless chicken
    breasts, cut into thirds
8 tomatoes, chopped
2 stalks celery, sliced
1/2 green pepper, sliced
1/4 c. burgundy cooking wine
    or chicken broth

4-1/2 oz. jar sliced mushrooms,
    drained
1 T. dried basil
salt and pepper to taste
1 T. cornstarch
1/4 c. cold water
cooked rice or pasta

In a skillet over medium heat, cook onion and garlic in butter until
tender and golden, about 5 minutes. Transfer to a slow cooker; add
remaining ingredients except cornstarch, water and rice or pasta. Cover
and cook on low setting for 5 hours. If desired, thicken sauce by
dissolving cornstarch in cold water; stir into mixture. Set slow cooker
to high setting and cook for 15 to 20 minutes, until thickened. Serve
chicken and sauce ladled over rice or pasta. Serves 4 to 6.

Keep bugs away from your cool
glasses of lemonade...simply
poke a hole through a paper
cupcake liner, add a straw,
flip it upside-down and use it
as a beverage cap. So clever!

Tummy-Pleasing Pizza Pasta

Margie Kirkman
High Point, NC

I tossed this together because I wanted something a little different...and something that wouldn't heat up the house!

1-1/2 lbs. ground beef
1 onion, chopped
16-oz. pkg. rigatoni pasta,
    cooked
4 c. shredded mozzarella cheese
2 14-oz. cans pizza sauce
Optional: 1 c. sliced mushrooms
8-oz. pkg. sliced pepperoni

In a skillet over medium heat, brown beef with onion; drain. In a slow cooker, alternate layers of beef mixture, pasta, cheese, sauce, mushrooms, if using, and pepperoni. Cover and cook on low setting for 4 to 5 hours. Serves 6.

Summer afternoon ... summer afternoon;
to me those have always been the two
most beautiful words in the English language.

–Henry James

Fettuccine & Pepperoni

Jean Yeager
New Castle, PA

*I often make this recipe when we're camping...I just use
a can of evaporated milk in place of the cream. We love
this simple and budget-friendly dish!*

4 eggs
1/4 c. whipping cream or
    5-oz. can evaporated milk
16-oz. pkg. fettuccine pasta,
    cooked

1/2 c. butter, softened
8-oz. pkg. sliced pepperoni
1 c. grated Parmesan cheese
1/4 c. fresh parsley, chopped

In a bowl, beat together eggs and cream or milk until well blended.
In a slow cooker, toss warm pasta with butter and pepperoni. Pour egg
mixture over top; stir. Cover and cook on low setting for 4 to 6 hours,
until set. Before serving, sprinkle with Parmesan cheese and parsley.
Serves 6 to 8.

Mmm...fresh air always makes us hungry! Slow-cooker suppers
are perfect for RV camping. Save time by chopping the veggies
at home, or choose a recipe with mostly canned ingredients.
Don't forget the can opener!

Fiesta Chicken Tacos

Lynnette Jones
East Flat Rock, NC

This simple recipe is so easy...you just put everything
in the slow cooker and let it go!

2 boneless, skinless chicken
  breasts
1-1/4 oz. pkg. taco seasoning
  mix
2 10-oz. cans diced tomatoes
  with green chiles

15-oz. can black beans, drained
  and rinsed
10 flour tortillas
Garnish: shredded cheese, sliced
  jalapeño peppers, shredded
  lettuce, diced tomatoes

Place chicken in a slow cooker; sprinkle with seasoning. Add tomatoes
with juice and beans. Cover and cook on low setting for 6 to 8 hours.
Shred chicken with 2 forks; stir to combine with mixture in slow
cooker. Fill tortillas with chicken mixture; add desired toppings.
Serves 4 to 6.

Chicken & Black Beans

Marissa Gurganious
Moreno Valley, CA

I wanted to share a recipe that my husband and I just love!

4 to 5 boneless, skinless chicken
  breasts
15-oz. can black beans, drained
  and rinsed

15-oz. can corn, drained
16-oz. jar salsa
8-oz. pkg. cream cheese, cubed

Place chicken in a slow cooker. Add beans and corn; pour salsa over
top. Cover and cook on high setting for 4 hours. Add cream cheese.
Cover and cook on high for 30 minutes longer, or until cream cheese
melts. Stir sauce before serving. Serves 4 to 5.

For high-altitude cooking, add an additional 30 minutes for
each hour of time specified in a slow-cooker recipe. Dried beans
can take up to twice as long to cook as they would at sea level.

Skinny Italian Creamy Chicken

Julie Pak
Henryetta, OK

My family loves cream cheese, so I'm constantly experimenting with it in my recipes. They also love any dish we can serve over rice or noodles. This is a huge hit in our house!

6 boneless, skinless chicken
  breasts
.7-oz. pkg. Italian salad dressing
  mix
1/3 c. warm water
8-oz. pkg. reduced-fat cream
  cheese, softened

1/2 c. plain yogurt
10-3/4 oz. can reduced-fat
  cream of chicken soup
1/2 c. shredded Parmesan
  cheese
cooked rice or pasta

Spray a large slow cooker with non-stick vegetable spray. Place chicken in slow cooker. In a small bowl, whisk together salad dressing mix and warm water; pour over chicken. In a separate bowl, beat together cream cheese, yogurt and soup; spoon over chicken. Sprinkle with Parmesan cheese. Cover and cook on low setting for 6 to 8 hours. Serve over rice or pasta. Serves 6.

Set a plump pillar candle in an old-fashioned punched tin lantern, and enjoy a soft glow on a warm summer night.

Crockery Minestrone

Denise Webb
Savannah, GA

We love soup...and this one is so easy, so delicious and makes the house smell so good while it cooks. It's one of our favorites!

1/2 lb. sweet Italian pork
   sausage links, sliced
1 t. olive oil
28-oz. can diced tomatoes
15-oz. can cannellini beans,
   drained and rinsed
15-oz. can kidney beans,
   drained and rinsed
6 carrots, peeled and chopped
4 stalks celery, chopped

1 onion, chopped
6 sprigs fresh thyme
1/2 t. dried sage
2 bay leaves
1/2 t. salt
1/2 t. pepper
8 c. chicken broth
2 c. ditalini pasta, uncooked
Garnish: grated Parmesan
   cheese

In a skillet over medium heat, brown sausage in oil. Add sausage to a slow cooker; add tomatoes with juice and remaining ingredients except pasta. Cover and cook on low setting for 7 to 8 hours. About 20 minutes before serving, cook pasta according to package directions; drain. Add pasta to slow cooker. Cover and cook for 20 to 30 minutes longer. Remove bay leaves before serving. Ladle soup into bowls; garnish with Parmesan cheese. Serves 12 to 15.

I have never had so many good ideas day after day
as when I worked in the garden.

–John Erskine

Rose Ciccone's Spaghetti Gravy

Diane Tracy
Lake Mary, FL

This is my mom's recipe that I've adapted for the slow cooker. She and my dad raised four daughters. My mom definitely knew how to make yummy food on a tight budget. It wasn't until I became a mom of five that I learned just how far a pound of spaghetti goes!

2 28-oz. cans whole tomatoes
12-oz. can tomato paste
1/2 green pepper, diced
1/2 red onion, diced
2 cloves garlic, diced

1-1/2 t. dried oregano
1 t. dried basil
2 bay leaves
salt and pepper to taste
1 T. brown sugar, packed

Place tomatoes with juice in a slow cooker; crush tomatoes with a potato masher until they are pulpy. Add remaining ingredients. Cover and cook on low setting for 5 to 8 hours. Remove bay leaf before serving. Serves 8 to 10.

Hearty Vegetarian Pasta Sauce

Meredith Martin
Austin, MN

I use carrots and zucchini fresh from the garden in this recipe, but the sweet potato baby food is the secret to this great sauce. If you are trying to disguise the high vegetable content, peel the zucchini before you grate it. It will just disappear!

2 28-oz. jars pasta sauce
4-oz. jar strained sweet potato
   baby food
1 c. carrot, peeled and grated

1 c. zucchini, grated
garlic powder, Italian seasoning
   and cayenne pepper to taste

Add pasta sauce and baby food to a slow cooker; stir to mix. Add remaining ingredients. Cover and cook on low setting for 2 to 4 hours. Serves 10.

Grate extra zucchini and freeze it in 2-cup portions...it'll be ready to add to your favorite recipes all winter long!

Spicy Bean & Turkey Sausage Stew

Ronda Hauss
Louisville, KY

This recipe is perfect for putting in the slow cooker in the morning and spending all day out boating on the lake. When we come back to the camp, dinner is done!

1 lb. smoked turkey sausage, halved lengthwise and sliced
16-oz. can kidney beans, drained and rinsed
15-oz. can Great Northern beans, drained and rinsed
15-oz. can black beans, drained and rinsed
1 onion, chopped

3 cloves garlic, minced
1 red pepper, chopped
1-1/2 c. frozen corn
16-oz. jar salsa
1 c. water
1 t. ground cumin
1/2 t. pepper
hot pepper sauce to taste

In a 5-quart slow cooker, combine all ingredients. Cover and cook on low setting for 6 to 8 hours. Stir before serving. Serves 6.

Dairy products like sour cream, milk and yogurt tend to break down during extended cooking. To prevent this, add them during the last 15 minutes of cooking.

Last-Resort Chicken Legs

Teri Tarrant
Newfoundland, Canada

Give the grill a break, and whip up these spicy, saucy barbecued chicken legs in the slow cooker!

6 to 10 chicken drumsticks
1/2 c. butter, sliced
1 T. onion salt or onion powder
1 T. garlic salt or garlic powder

1 t. pepper
1/4 c. hot pepper sauce
3/4 c. barbecue sauce
1/2 c. water

Place drumsticks in a deep skillet, cover with water. Over high heat, simmer drumsticks until just cooked; drain. Transfer to a slow cooker; add remaining ingredients. Cover and cook on high setting for 2 hours, stirring once or twice. Reduce heat to low. Cover and cook on low setting for up to 2 hours longer, or until ready to serve. Serves 2 to 3.

A summer snack that's oh-so refreshing...dip hulled strawberries in thick Greek yogurt, then place on a baking sheet lined with parchment or wax paper. Freeze until solid.

Barbecued Beef Brisket

Judy Weyer
Cincinnati, OH

Tender slices of slow-cooked beef brisket are topped with a sweet and savory sauce...yum! It's a perfect recipe for when you're craving barbecue but want to take a break from the grill.

3-lb. beef brisket
1-1/2 t. coarse salt
3/4 t. pepper
1 T. oil
1-1/2 c. onion, coarsely chopped
1-1/2 T. garlic, minced
1/2 c. dark beer or beef broth

1 T. Worcestershire sauce
2 T. lemon juice
3 T. honey
1/2 c. catsup
1 t. paprika
12 kaiser sandwich rolls, split

Rub brisket with salt and pepper on all sides. Heat oil in a large skillet over medium-high heat. Add brisket; brown on all sides. Transfer to a large slow cooker. In a bowl, combine remaining ingredients except rolls; spoon over brisket. Cover and cook on low setting for 8 hours, or until brisket is very tender. Remove brisket from slow cooker. Place on a cutting board; let it rest for 15 minutes. Slice brisket thinly; divide it among rolls. Top with some sauce from the slow cooker. Serve warm. Serves 8 to 10.

Cooking for a crowd? Roasting meats can easily be doubled in a large slow cooker. Add only half as much seasoning for the doubled portion, not twice as much...otherwise flavors may be too strong.

Summer Berry Cobbler

JoAnn

Serve warm topped with whipped cream or ice cream...a delectable summer dessert best enjoyed on the front porch at the day's end, listening to a chorus of crickets for entertainment.

5 c. mixed berries, such as
    raspberries, blueberries,
    blackberries or strawberries
1 c. sugar, divided
2-3/4 c. biscuit baking mix,
    divided

1/4 c. butter, melted
1/2 c. milk
2 t. cinnamon

Spray a slow cooker with non-stick vegetable spray. In a large bowl, toss together berries, 1/2 cup sugar and 1/2 cup baking mix. Transfer mixture to slow cooker. In another bowl, stir together remaining baking mix, 1/4 cup remaining sugar, melted butter and milk until a soft dough forms. Using your hands, drop dollops of dough on top of berries in the slow cooker. In a small bowl, stir together remaining sugar and cinnamon; sprinkle over dough. Do not stir. Cover and cook on high setting for 2 to 2-1/2 hours, until dough is puffy and fruit is bubbly. Serves 8 to 10.

It's easy to save summer's fresh berries to enjoy later. Simply arrange berries in a single layer on a baking sheet and freeze, then store in plastic freezer bags. Frozen this way, it's convenient to remove just the amount of berries you need. Frozen berries may be added directly to a baked recipe...just increase the baking time by about 10 minutes.

Slow Peach Cobbler

Laurel Perry
Loganville, GA

This is a great dessert to share at potlucks! People won't believe that it was made in a slow cooker.

1/3 c. sugar
1/2 c. brown sugar, packed
3/4 c. biscuit baking mix
2 eggs, beaten
2 t. vanilla extract

2 t. butter, melted
3/4 c. evaporated milk
3 to 4 peaches, peeled, chopped
  and lightly mashed
3/4 t. cinnamon

Spray a slow cooker with non-stick vegetable spray. In a large bowl, combine sugars and baking mix. Add eggs, vanilla, butter and milk; stir well. Fold in peaches and cinnamon. Pour into slow cooker. Cover and cook on low setting for 6 to 8 hours, or on high setting for 3 to 4 hours. Serve warm. Serves 6 to 8.

Think flea-market fresh when decorating the kitchen for summer. Fill an enamelware colander with fresh fruit or veggies from the garden...a vintage child-size watering can is the perfect size for just-picked garden blooms.

Slow & Easy Summer

Easy-Peasy Berry Cobbler

Jessica Zelkovich
Hamilton, IL

*You'll love this super-simple and delicious dessert...
there's only four ingredients!*

16-oz. pkg. frozen mixed berries
1/2 c. sugar

12-oz. tube refrigerated biscuits
cinnamon to taste

Pour frozen berries into a slow cooker; stir in sugar. Arrange biscuits on top; sprinkle with cinnamon. Cover and cook on high setting for 3 hours. Serve warm. Serves 6 to 8.

Easy Blueberry Dessert

Susan Bick
Ballwin, MO

Just as delicious if you substitute cherry or apple pie filling!

21-oz. can blueberry pie filling
18-1/2 oz. pkg. yellow cake mix
1/2 c. butter, melted

1/3 c. chopped walnuts
Garnish: vanilla ice cream

Place pie filling in a lightly greased slow cooker. In a bowl, combine dry cake mix and butter. Mixture will be crumbly. Sprinkle over pie filling. Sprinkle with walnuts. Cover and cook on low setting for 4 hours, or on high setting for 2 hours. Allow to cool slightly. To serve, scoop into bowls and top with ice cream. Serves 10 to 12.

Hot Fudge Sundae Cake

Gloria Robertson
Midland, TX

Surprise! This cake creates its own gooey hot fudge sauce.
Scoop it up and enjoy.

1 c. all-purpose flour
1/2 c. sugar
6 T. baking cocoa, divided
2 t. baking powder
1/2 t. salt
1/2 c. milk

2 T. oil
1 t. vanilla extract
1/2 c. chopped nuts
3/4 c. brown sugar, packed
1-1/2 c. hot water

Spray a 2 to 3-quart slow cooker with non-stick vegetable spray. In a bowl, stir together flour, sugar, 2 tablespoons baking cocoa, baking powder and salt. Stir in milk, oil and vanilla. Fold in nuts. Spread batter evenly in slow cooker. In a separate bowl, combine brown sugar and remaining baking cocoa; stir in hot water until smooth. Pour evenly over batter in slow cooker. Do not stir. Cover and cook on high setting for 2 to 2-1/2 hours, until a toothpick inserted in center comes out clean. Turn off slow cooker. Let cake stand, uncovered, for 30 to 40 minutes before serving. Spoon warm cake into dessert dishes; spoon sauce from slow cooker over top. Serves 6 to 8.

Slow cookers are perfect party helpers! Just plug them in and they'll keep food bubbly and yummy with no effort at all.

Kathy's Favorite Chocolate Sauce
Teisha Priest
Lee, ME

This is my mom's favorite recipe for homemade chocolate sauce. Mom made hers in a double boiler, but I make mine in my trusty slow cooker. The large batch makes it easy to give some away and still have plenty for your own family to enjoy. It keeps very well in the fridge.

1 c. butter, sliced
6 1-oz. sqs. unsweetened
    baking chocolate
5 c. sugar, divided

2 12-oz. cans evaporated milk
1 t. salt
2 t. vanilla extract

Add butter and chocolate to a slow cooker. Cook, uncovered, on high setting until butter and chocolate melt, stirring constantly. Gradually add sugar, 1/2 cup at a time, stirring well after each addition. Gradually stir in evaporated milk; mix well. Stir in salt and vanilla. Cover and cook on low setting for 1-1/2 to 2 hours. Refrigerate in a covered container. Makes 2 quarts.

Add a touch of whimsy...use Mom's old cow-shaped milk pitcher to top desserts with chocolate sauce or cream.

Chocolate Pudding Cake

Darcy Ericksen
Independence, MO

This is such an easy treat to whip up...and I almost always have the ingredients on hand.

3 c. milk
3.4-oz. pkg. cook & serve
   chocolate pudding mix
18-1/2 oz. pkg. chocolate cake
   mix

Garnish: frozen whipped
   topping, thawed

In a bowl, whisk together milk and dry pudding mix. Pour into a slow cooker that has been sprayed with non-stick vegetable spray; set aside. Prepare cake mix according to package directions; carefully pour batter into slow cooker. Do not stir. Cover and cook on high setting for 2-1/2 hours, or until cake is set. Serve warm with whipped topping. Makes 8 to 12 servings.

Serving ice cream at your backyard gathering? Here's an easy no-drip solution. Before the guests arrive, place individual scoops in a muffin tin lined with paper baking cups. Transfer to the freezer for up to several hours. So easy!

Chocolate Raspberry Strata

Jill Ross
Pickerington, OH

Rich chocolate and red raspberries always make a winning combination. Save a few fresh raspberries to garnish individual servings...so elegant!

6 c. brioche or challah bread, cubed
1-1/2 c. semi-sweet chocolate chips
1/2 pt. fresh raspberries

1/2 c. whipping cream
1/2 c. milk
4 eggs, beaten
1/4 c. sugar
1 t. vanilla extract

Place half of bread cubes in a slow cooker. Sprinkle with half of chocolate chips and raspberries. Repeat layering. In a bowl, whisk together remaining ingredients; pour over top. Cover and cook on high setting for 1-1/2 to 2 hours. Serves 10.

A festive table runner for any occasion can be as simple as a roll of gift wrapping paper. Just unroll along the table's length; secure ends if needed. At the party's end, just throw it away!

Mock Apple Butter

Patricia Coulter
Canmer, KY

An Amish friend shared this recipe with me after hearing me comment about the abundance of zucchini we had last summer. Now I make this version instead of using my backyard apples...I save those for apple pie filling and applesauce!

8 c. zucchini, peeled, seeded and
    diced
12-oz. can frozen apple juice
    concentrate
1 c. sugar

1 t. cinnamon
1/2 c. red cinnamon candies
5 1-pint canning jars and lids,
    sterilized

Combine all ingredients in a slow cooker; mix well. Cover and cook on low setting for 8 to 10 hours. Transfer mixture to a blender or food processor; purée until smooth. Ladle hot mixture into hot sterilized jars, leaving 1/2-inch headspace. Wipe rims; secure with lids and rings. Process in a boiling water bath for 10 minutes. Set jars on a towel to cool; check for seals. Makes about 5 pints.

Enamelware is often cast off if it has a rusty hole in the bottom. But before tossing those colorful pieces, give them a new life! Filled with potting soil and colorful summertime annuals, they bring a touch of whimsy to any porch.

Hearty Harvest Favorites

Special-Morning Oatmeal

Gladys Kielar
Perrysburg, OH

*Breakfast is ready when you wake up! My mother made this
tummy-warming oatmeal for our birthday breakfasts and
other special occasions. We always looked forward to it.*

1/3 c. brown sugar, packed
2 t. cinnamon
1 t. nutmeg
2 apples, peeled, cored and
    thinly sliced
3/4 c. sweetened dried
    cranberries

1/4 c. butter, sliced
2 c. old-fashioned oats,
    uncooked
2 c. water
1 c. apple juice
1 c. cranberry juice cocktail

In a bowl, mix brown sugar, cinnamon and nutmeg. Add apples and
cranberries; toss to coat. Transfer to a slow cooker; dot with butter.
Combine oats, water and juices; pour over fruit mixture in slow cooker.
Do not stir. Cover and cook on low setting for 8 hours. Stir before
serving. Serves 4.

Cook up a crock of overnight grits...creamy and perfect
every time! Following the package directions, add the desired
amount of grits to a slow cooker (long-cooking grits work
best) and twice the amount of water as specified. Sprinkle with
salt. Cover and cook on low setting for 7 to 8 hours, stirring in
more water toward the end of cooking time, if needed. Top
with butter, shredded cheese or a splash of cream.

Cinnamon-Ginger Pears

JoAnn

*Tender, slow-cooked pears are delicious paired with
rich vanilla Greek yogurt.*

3 c. boiling water
1 c. sugar
1/4 c. fresh ginger, peeled and
   chopped
2 4-inch cinnamon sticks

zest and juice of 2 lemons
5 to 6 pears, peeled, halved
   and cored
Garnish: vanilla Greek yogurt

Pour boiling water into a slow cooker; stir in sugar, ginger, cinnamon
sticks, lemon zest and juice. Place pears into hot liquid in the slow
cooker. Cover and cook on low setting for 3 to 4 hours, or on high
setting for one to 2 hours, until pears are tender. Discard lemon zest
and cinnamon sticks. Serve pears over a serving of yogurt; drizzle with
some sauce from the slow cooker. Makes 5 to 6 servings.

Always turn your slow cooker off, unplug it from the
electrical outlet and allow it to cool before cleaning. The
outside of the heating base may be cleaned with
a soft cloth and warm soapy water.

Grandma's Old-Fashioned Fruit Compote

Debrah Veronese
Bend, OR

This warm fruit is delicious spooned over yogurt or oatmeal.
Served over ice cream, it's yummy enough for dessert, too!

4 apples, peeled, cored and
    cut into chunks
4 pears, peeled, cored and
    cut into chunks
1 c. raisins
1 c. fresh cranberries
1 c. fresh or frozen blackberries
1 c. sugar
2 t. cinnamon

1 t. nutmeg
1 t. cardamom
1/2 c. water
13-1/2 oz. can sliced peaches
    in syrup
15-oz. can apricot halves in juice
14-1/2 oz. can pitted sweet
    cherries, drained

Place all ingredients except canned fruits in a slow cooker; stir well. Cover and cook on low setting for 4 to 6 hours. Add canned fruits with syrup and juice; cover and cook for one additional hour. Stir well before serving. Serve warm. Makes 20 to 24 servings.

October is crisp days and cool nights,
a time to curl up around the dancing flames
and sink into a good book.

–John Sinor

Harvest Apple Butter

Lisa Ann Panzino DiNunzio
Vineland, NJ

My mom makes this apple butter often. It's the most delicious apple butter I've ever had. It goes quickly...so, before you know it, she's making another batch!

14 to 16 Granny Smith apples,
   peeled, cored and quartered
1/2 c. dark brown sugar, packed
1/2 c. apple cider

1 T. cinnamon
1 T. lemon juice
1/8 t. ground cloves

Add all ingredients to a slow cooker; mix well. Cover and cook on low setting for 8 hours. Uncover; mash apples and cook, uncovered, for 2 hours longer, stirring occasionally. Allow mixture to cool; store in an airtight container in the refrigerator. Makes about 3 cups.

Host a backyard bonfire weenie roast in the fall when the weather turns cool & crisp. Fill a couple of slow cookers with hearty baked beans and simmering spiced cider. Don't forget the s'more fixin's!

Game-Day Sausage Rolls

*Renee Bailey
Tomah, WI*

*My mom always made this game-day favorite, and it's still
a favorite with my family today! It's a perfect sandwich to
enjoy on those cool-weather football Sundays.*

6 smoked pork bratwursts,
    cut into thirds
6 smoked hot Italian pork
    sausages, cut into thirds
1 onion, sliced
1 to 2 green peppers, sliced

2 4-oz. cans sliced mushrooms,
    drained
26-oz. jar spaghetti sauce
12 hot dog buns or sub rolls,
    split
2 c. shredded mozzarella cheese

Pan-fry or grill sausages until lightly browned. Add sausages, onion,
peppers, mushrooms and sauce to a slow cooker. Cover and cook on
low setting for 4 to 6 hours, until vegetables are tender. Serve on buns;
top with cheese. Makes 12 servings.

No peeking! Lifting the lid on the slow cooker allows heat
and moisture to escape and can delay cooking time by
15 to 20 minutes. Just remove the lid when stirring and
adding ingredients as specified by the recipe.

Club Sandwich Dip

Patricia Stagich
Elizabeth, NJ

I like to serve this tasty dip with rye toast points...
just like a good deli sandwich!

1 lb. deli turkey, chopped
1/2 lb. deli ham, chopped
1/2 lb. sliced Swiss or American
   cheese, chopped
8-oz. pkg. cream cheese, cubed
1 c. mayonnaise
2 t. Dijon mustard

6 slices bacon, crisply cooked
   and crumbled
1/2 c. cherry or grape tomatoes,
   chopped
toast points and assorted cut
   veggies

In a 4-quart slow cooker, combine turkey, ham, cheeses, mayonnaise and mustard. Cover and cook on high setting for one to 2 hours, until cheeses are melted, stirring after one hour. Before serving, stir in half of the bacon; garnish with remaining bacon and tomatoes. Serve warm with toast points and veggies. Serves 20.

Serve up a Bucket O'Bones at your next tailgate party!
Press a mini marshmallow into each end of a pretzel stick
and roll in melted white chocolate.

Buffalo Chicken Dip

Donna Lewis
Ostrander, OH

It just wouldn't be a party without everyone's favorite dip!

2 8-oz. pkgs. cream cheese
1 c. ranch salad dressing
1 c. buffalo wing sauce
3 boneless, skinless chicken
   breasts, cooked and
   shredded

1 c. shredded Mexican-blend
   cheese
tortilla chips

In a slow cooker, combine cream cheese, salad dressing and wing sauce. Cover and cook on high setting for one to 2 hours. When cream cheese is melted and mixture is creamy, stir in chicken and shredded cheese. Cover and cook until heated through. Before serving, turn slow cooker to low setting. Serve warm with tortilla chips. Serves 10 to 12.

Easy Chicken Chili

Mary Little
Franklin, TN

Our family loves to enjoy this dish on a chilly Tennessee evening.

2 to 3 5-oz. cans chicken
3 15-oz. cans Great Northern
   beans
2 15-1/2 oz. cans hominy

16-oz. jar salsa
2 8-oz. pkgs. shredded
   Monterey Jack cheese

Combine all ingredients in a slow cooker, including liquid from cans. Cover and cook on low setting for 8 hours. Serves 8 to 10.

Penny Social Pulled Pork

Karen Couch
Palm Bay, FL

I make this very easy and tasty pulled pork every time
we have a Penny Social fundraising event at our school.
It's always a favorite.

1 yellow onion, chopped
3-lb. boneless pork loin
2 T. garlic, minced

32-oz. container beef broth
18-oz. bottle barbecue sauce
16 sandwich buns

Place onion, pork, garlic and broth in a large slow cooker. Cover and
cook on high setting for 6 to 7 hours, until pork is fork-tender. Drain
slow cooker; shred pork with 2 forks. Add barbecue sauce, a little at a
time, until you have it as saucy as you want. Reduce temperature to
low setting. Serve on buns with additional sauce, if desired. Makes
16 servings.

Rolls and buns filled with juicy, slow-cooked meat
will drip less if they're toasted first.

Italian Beef in a Bucket

Carol Bobeng
Raleigh, NC

This is a family favorite and is a "must" at every gathering. My son makes it, my daughter makes it and last time, my oldest grandson prepared it. Hope it becomes a favorite in your family, too!

3-1/2 to 4-lb. beef rump roast
12-oz. jar Italian giardiniera
   mix, mild or hot, drained
12-oz. jar pepperoncini

.7-oz. pkg. zesty Italian salad
   dressing mix
10-1/2 oz. can beef broth
12 to 18 crusty Italian rolls

Place beef roast in a large slow cooker. In a bowl, combine remaining ingredients except rolls; do not drain pepperoncini. Pour mixture over roast. Cover and cook on low setting for 10 to 12 hours, until meat is very tender. Shred with 2 forks; stir into mixture in slow cooker. Serve on rolls; top with some of the giardiniera mixture from the slow cooker. Makes 12 to 18 servings.

Serve up hot & tasty sandwiches at your next tailgating party...right out of a slow cooker! Plug it into a power inverter that draws from your car battery.

Kimmy's Amazing Black Bean Chili-Cheese Dip

Kim Ralston
Murfreesboro, TN

This festive dip is my go-to dip for any get-together! It freezes wonderfully too, so you can make it in advance.

1 lb. ground beef
1 lb. ground pork sausage
32-oz. pkg. pasteurized process
   cheese spread, cubed
8-oz. pkg. cream cheese, cubed
2 15-1/2 oz. cans black beans,
   drained and rinsed

3 14-1/2 oz. cans fire-roasted
   diced tomatoes
6 T. taco seasoning mix
1-oz. pkg. fiesta ranch dip mix
assorted dippers, such as
   tortilla chips, corn chips
   and cut veggies

In a skillet over medium heat, brown beef and sausage until crumbled and no longer pink; drain. To a 6 to 7-quart slow cooker, add cheeses, beans and tomatoes with juice. Add beef mixture. Sprinkle with seasoning mixes; stir well. Cover and cook on low setting for 2 hours, stirring every 20 minutes, until cheeses are melted and dip is warmed through. Turn slow cooker to warm setting; serve with dippers. Serves 24.

For an easy weeknight dinner or perfect party fare, just combine one jar spaghetti sauce, one cup water and one pound frozen meatballs in a slow cooker. Cover and cook on low setting for 6 to 8 hours. Serve meatballs on toasted rolls; top with shredded mozzarella cheese. Yum!

Pleasing Pizza Dip

Jennifer Crisp
Abingdon, IL

This recipe goes so fast that I have to put out two slow cookers for our family gatherings! You can toss in any of your favorite pizza toppings, and it will be delicious.

1 c. ground Italian pork sausage, browned and drained
1 c. pepperoni, diced
2 8-oz. pkgs. cream cheese, cubed
2 c. shredded Cheddar cheese
1-1/2 c. sour cream
2-1/2 c. pizza sauce
2 to 3 T. dried oregano
2 t. garlic powder
tortilla chips

Combine all ingredients except tortilla chips in a slow cooker. Cover and cook on low setting for 2 hours, stirring occasionally, until dip is smooth and warmed through. Serve warm with tortilla chips. Serves 10 to 12.

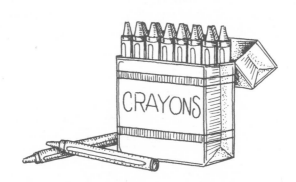

Muffin-tin crayons...a fun rainy day activity for kids! Gather some broken crayons and a mini muffin tin or candy mold that will fit in your slow cooker. Remove wrappers and break crayons into small pieces. Mound up pieces in muffin cups and place tin in slow cooker. Cover and cook on high setting for one to 2 hours, until wax is completely melted. Turn off slow cooker; let stand until wax begins to harden. Transfer to refrigerator and cool for 30 minutes longer.

Party Corn Dip

Whitney Burgess
Florence, AL

This is my go-to recipe for any party. It's so simple, fast and always a crowd-pleaser!

3 15-oz. cans shoepeg corn
3 10-oz. cans diced tomatoes
   with green chiles

3 8-oz. pkgs. cream cheese,
   cubed
corn chips

Partially drain each can of corn and tomatoes, leaving about half the liquid in each can. Pour corn and tomatoes with remaining liquid into a slow cooker; add cream cheese. Cover and cook on low setting for one to 2 hours, stirring occasionally, until cream cheese is melted and dip is warmed through. Serve warm with corn chips for dipping. Serves 8 to 10.

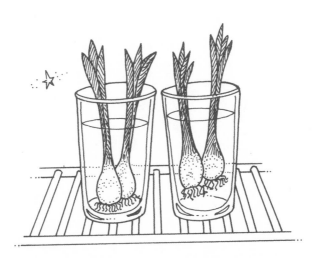

Keep green onions fresh longer by storing them bulb-ends down in a half-full glass of water in the refrigerator. Change the water every few days.

Honey-Chipotle Pulled Pork

Carol Patterson
Deltona, FL

This slow-cooker pulled pork is easy and delicious. Chipotle peppers in adobo sauce combined with honey create a delicious sweet-heat combination that is guaranteed to be a hit!

3 lbs. boneless pork chops or
    pork roast
1 c. catsup

3/4 c. honey
2 canned chipotle peppers in
    adobo sauce, chopped

Place pork in a lightly greased slow cooker. Cover and cook on low setting for 8 hours. Drain liquid and remove fat, if needed. Shred pork with 2 forks. In a bowl, combine catsup, honey and chipotle peppers; pour over pork. Stir to combine; warm through. Serves 8 to 10.

Got leftovers? Transfer cooked food to smaller storage containers before you refrigerate it. Because the ceramic insert is so thick and dense, the food won't cool down quickly enough for safety.

Rockin' Ribs

Susan Buetow
Du Quoin, IL

I never used to like ribs, so I never made them. On the other hand, my husband has always loved ribs. One year, I decided to make him the best ribs ever for his birthday. They were so good, I even converted myself into a rib lover! My husband and kids all love this recipe, and so does anyone else who tries it.

1 c. brown sugar, packed
6 cloves garlic, minced
1/4 c. smoke-flavored cooking
    sauce
3 slabs pork baby back ribs,
    each cut into thirds

1 onion, thinly sliced
1 ltr. cola
Garnish: favorite-flavor
    barbecue sauce

In a bowl, mix brown sugar, garlic and cooking sauce. Coat each rib piece with brown sugar mixture; stack in a large slow cooker, laying onion slices between ribs. Spoon any remaining brown sugar mixture over top; pour cola over everything. Cover and cook on high setting for 6 to 8 hours, until ribs are tender. Serve with barbecue sauce. Serves 4 to 6.

No need to heat up the kitchen on a warm Indian summer day. Did you know you can bake potatoes in your slow cooker? In the morning, simply pierce potatoes with a fork and wrap in aluminum foil. Cover and cook on low setting for 8 to 10 hours...ready by dinnertime!

Spinach-Artichoke Dip

Denise Winder
Old Fort, TN

*This dip was a favorite of all the girls I worked with.
It's truly a no-fail recipe...you'll love it!*

2 8-oz. pkgs. cream cheese,
    softened
1/3 c. grated Parmesan cheese
3/4 c. whipping cream
1/4 t. garlic powder
16-oz. pkg. frozen chopped
    spinach, thawed and drained

14-oz. can artichoke hearts,
    drained and chopped
2/3 c. shredded Monterey Jack
    cheese
tortilla chips

In a bowl, combine cream cheese, Parmesan cheese, cream and garlic
powder; mix well. Fold in spinach and artichokes. Transfer mixture to
a slow cooker that has been sprayed with non-stick vegetable spray.
Spread evenly. Cover and cook on high setting for one to 1-1/2 hours,
until bubbly around the edges. Sprinkle with shredded cheese. Cover
and cook on low setting for 15 minutes longer, or until cheese is
melted. Serve warm with tortilla chips. Serves 10.

Cayenne pepper and hot pepper sauce tend to become
bitter if cooked for long periods of time. Use small amounts
and add toward the end of the cooking time.

Aunt Barb's Dip

Brittney Green
Frederick, CO

This dip has been a favorite in our family for years...everyone just loves it! It's perfect for fall football parties. You can easily double the recipe, and you very well may need to.

1-1/2 lbs. ground beef
1 onion, chopped
1 green pepper, chopped
1 T. chili powder
14-1/2 oz. can stewed tomatoes
15-oz. can ranch-style pinto
   beans with jalapeños

10-3/4 oz. can cream of chicken
   soup
10-3/4 oz. can cream of
   mushroom soup
16-oz. pkg. pasteurized process
   cheese spread, cubed
tortilla chips

In a skillet over medium heat, brown beef with onion and green pepper; drain. Sprinkle with chili powder. Transfer beef mixture to a large slow cooker; add undrained tomatoes, undrained beans and remaining ingredients except tortilla chips. Stir well. Cover and cook on low setting for 4 hours, stirring occasionally, until cheese melts and dip is warmed through. Serve warm with tortilla chips. Serves 20.

Your slow cooker makes a great server for hot beverages or dips. Keep it on the low setting to maintain the proper serving temperature.

Slow-Cooker Turkey Chili

Barbie Hall
Salisbury, MD

My husband and I quickly invented this chili recipe one morning when we knew we had a very busy day ahead of us. He arrived home in time to make some cornbread muffins too. What a wonderful meal to come home to!

2 lbs. ground turkey
2 onions, chopped
3 cloves garlic, minced
28-oz. can diced tomatoes
28-oz. can tomato purée
15-1/2 oz. can kidney beans,
    drained and rinsed

15-1/2 oz. can chili beans
2-1/2 T. chili powder
1 T. ground cumin
1/2 t. cayenne pepper
1 t. salt

In a skillet over medium heat, brown turkey; drain. Transfer to a slow cooker, reserving 2 tablespoons drippings in the skillet. In the same skillet, cook onions until translucent. Add garlic; cook for one minute longer. Add onion mixture and remaining ingredients to slow cooker; stir to combine. Cover and cook on low setting for 6 to 8 hours. Serves 8.

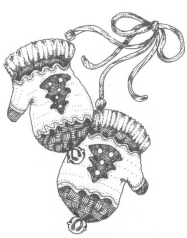

Share the warmth. With winter on the way, autumn is a perfect time to pull outgrown coats, hats and mittens out of closets and donate them to a local charity.

Ultimate White Chicken Chili

Sonda Huhta
Loveland, CO

*I often make this recipe for the annual harvest party
at my daughter's elementary school. It's enjoyed by
teachers, parents and children alike!*

2 14-1/2 oz. cans chicken broth
4 c. chicken, cooked and
  chopped
2 4-oz. cans chopped green
  chiles
3 15-oz. cans Great Northern
  beans, drained and rinsed

2 c. shredded Monterey Jack
  cheese
1/8 t. cayenne pepper
1 t. dried oregano
2-1/2 t. ground cumin
16-oz. container sour cream

Add all ingredients except sour cream to a slow cooker. Cover and cook
on low setting for 6 to 8 hours. Shortly before serving, stir in sour
cream; heat through. Serves 8.

Bright yellow, red, and orange,
The leaves come down in hosts;
The trees are Indian princes,
But soon they'll turn to ghosts.

–William Allingham

Basic Mexican Chicken

Julie Saifullah
Lexington, KY

I make this chicken often because it is so versatile. You can use it to make all kinds of Mexican dishes, like tacos, enchiladas, burritos, rice bowls, nachos or even chicken tortilla soup!

6 boneless, skinless chicken
   breasts
1-1/4 oz. pkg. taco seasoning
   mix

16-oz. jar salsa

Place chicken in a slow cooker; sprinkle with taco seasoning. Pour salsa over top; do not stir. Cover and cook on low setting for 8 hours. Shred chicken with 2 forks; mix well with sauce in slow cooker. Serves 6 to 8.

Try some shredded beef for tacos! Slow-cook a beef chuck roast with some chopped onion and Montreal steak seasoning on low setting for 8 hours. Shred with two forks and stir with sauce in slow cooker before serving.

Hot Turkey & Stuffing Sandwiches

Kendall Hale
Lynn, MA

All the comforting flavors of Thanksgiving in a warm, satisfying sandwich! This is a great way to use up leftover turkey too.

2 to 3 boneless, skinless turkey
   thighs, cubed
1 onion, chopped
1 stalk celery, chopped
1 carrot, peeled and chopped
14-oz. pkg. stuffing mix
2 c. chicken broth
12 sandwich buns, split

Add all ingredients except buns to a 3-1/2 to 4-quart slow cooker; stir well. Cover and cook on low setting for 8 to 9 hours. To serve, scoop about 1/2 cup turkey mixture onto each bun. Makes 12 servings.

Mini versions of favorite hot sandwiches are oh-so appealing on party platters...they help food stretch farther too! Try using small sandwich rolls or brown & serve dinner rolls instead of full-size buns.

Cheesy Sausage Dip

Debra Collins
Gaylesville, AL

This is an awesome dip for any party!

1 lb. ground pork sausage
8-oz. pkg. cream cheese, cubed
8-oz. container sour cream
10-oz. can diced tomatoes with
   green chiles

1 c. shredded Cheddar cheese
10-oz. pkg. frozen spinach,
   thawed and drained
1/2 t. garlic powder

In a skillet over medium heat, brown sausage; drain and set aside. In a slow cooker, combine cream cheese, sour cream, tomatoes with juice and Cheddar cheese. Cover and cook on low setting for one hour, or until cheeses are melted. Stir in spinach, sausage and garlic powder. Cover and cook on low setting for one to 2 hours longer, until dip is smooth and warmed through. Serves 10 to 15.

Hot Tomato-Cheese Dip

Beth Bennett
Stratham, NH

The mushroom soup is the "secret" ingredient...it really makes a difference.

16-oz. pkg. pasteurized process
   cheese spread, cubed
10-oz. can diced tomatoes with
   green chiles

10-3/4 oz. can cream of
   mushroom soup
assorted dippers, such as corn
   chips or sliced veggies

Combine all ingredients except dippers in a slow cooker. Cover and cook on low setting for one to 2 hours, until dip is smooth and warmed through. Serve warm with corn chips or veggies for dipping. Serves 10 to 12.

Cooking on low heat takes about twice as long as cooking on high heat. A general rule of thumb is that "low heat" means about 200 degrees and "high heat" is about 300 degrees.

Hot Apple Punch

Michelle Tucker
Hamilton, OH

*What a wonderful warm drink for autumn. Plus, it makes
your home smell simply delightful!*

2 qts. apple juice
1-1/2 c. cranberry juice cocktail
1/2 c. brown sugar, packed
1/2 t. salt

4 4-inch cinnamon sticks
2 whole cloves
Garnish: 1 orange, sliced

Combine all ingredients except orange slices in a slow cooker. Cover
and cook on low setting for 2 hours, or until brown sugar is dissolved
and mixture is hot. Strain cinnamon sticks and cloves before serving;
top with orange slices. Serves 12.

Sprinkle the inside of your Jack-o'-Lantern with
some pumpkin pie spice. It will smell delicious
when the candle is lit!

Caramel Apple Cider

Michelle Marberry
Valley, AL

*Tailgaters and trick-or-treaters love this drink
on a crisp fall night!*

64-oz. bottle apple cider
1/2 c. caramel ice cream topping
1/2 t. cinnamon

Garnish: whipped cream,
cinnamon, additional caramel
topping, cinnamon sticks

Combine all ingredients except garnish in a slow cooker. Cover and cook on low setting for 3 to 4 hours. Ladle hot cider into mugs; top with a dollop of whipped cream, a sprinkle of cinnamon and a drizzle of caramel topping. Serve with a cinnamon stick for stirring. Makes 8 servings.

Start your own Halloween dinner tradition! In the morning, put on a slow cooker of chili, beef stew or vegetable soup to simmer all day. It will be easy for everyone to grab a bowlful before putting on costumes or in between handing out treats.

Bacon-Wrapped Chicken

Jana Bailey
Zeeland, MI

My house smells so good while this chicken is cooking away in the slow cooker! Make sure your chicken is fully wrapped in the bacon.

1 lb. bacon, divided
1 lb. Brussels sprouts, peeled
   and chopped
1 c. baby carrots, chopped
1 c. celery, chopped
6 redskin potatoes, cubed

1 Granny Smith apple, cored and
   chopped
poultry seasoning and cracked
   pepper to taste
3 to 3-1/2 lb. whole chicken

In a skillet over medium heat, cook 4 slices bacon until crisp; drain, crumble and set aside. In a large bowl, combine vegetables, apple, herbs and pepper; stir in crumbled bacon. Stuff chicken with some of the vegetable mixture. Add remaining vegetable mixture to a large slow cooker; place stuffed chicken on top. Cover entire chicken with remaining slices of uncooked bacon. Cover and cook on low or medium setting for 8 to 9 hours, until chicken juices run clear when pierced with a fork. Serves 4 to 6.

On clear, crisp autumn days, freshen household quilts and blankets for winter. Simply shake them out and spread over a porch rail or fence. Sunshine and fresh air will quickly chase away any mustiness that they've picked up in storage.

Quick Pork Chops & Gravy

Carol Hickman
Kingsport, TN

This is a stand-by dinner for those busy days when I just don't have the time to put together a made-from-scratch meal. I toss the pork chops in the slow cooker before I leave for work, and when I get home I just heat up some green beans, frozen mashed potatoes and brown & serve dinner rolls for a stick-to-your-ribs meal in minutes!

2 12-oz. jars pork gravy
10-3/4 oz. can cream of
    mushroom soup

1.35-oz. pkg. onion soup mix
8 boneless pork chops
salt and pepper to taste

In a slow cooker, stir together gravy, soup and soup mix. In a large skillet generously sprayed with non-stick cooking spray, brown pork chops on both sides over medium-high heat; season with salt and pepper. Do not cook through. Place chops in slow cooker; press down until covered with gravy mixture. Cover and cook on high setting for 3 to 4 hours, or on low setting for 6 to 8 hours. Remove lid for the last hour of cooking to allow gravy to thicken. Makes 8 servings.

With work, school and after-school activities, dinner can
be a challenge. Now's the time to get out that slow cooker!
Other than a quick chop of a few ingredients, recipes are
usually a simple matter of tossing everything into the pot.

Harvest Stew

Cindy Wilsey
Marinette, WI

This recipe was shared by a friend of my mom's who lived on a family dairy farm. She used her slow cooker often...it made coordinating mealtimes on a busy farm a little bit easier!

1 lb. lean ground turkey, beef
   or chicken
1 acorn squash
14-1/2 oz. can diced tomatoes
16-oz. can kidney beans,
   drained and rinsed
4 c. chicken broth
1 yellow onion, chopped

3 cloves garlic, chopped
1 sweet potato, peeled and
   chopped
3 redskin potatoes, peeled
   and chopped
Optional: 1/4 t. allspice
salt and pepper to taste

In a skillet over medium heat, brown meat; drain and set aside. Microwave whole squash on high setting for 2 minutes; peel and chop. Add squash, meat, tomatoes with juice and remaining ingredients to a 6-1/2 quart slow cooker; stir well. Cover and cook on low setting for 7 to 9 hours. Serves 6 to 8.

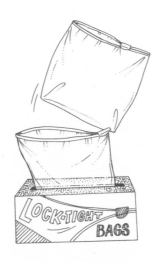

Jump-start tomorrow's dinner! Chop and assemble ingredients tonight...refrigerate meat and veggies in separate containers.

Creamy Butternut Squash Soup

Hope Comerford
Clinton Township, MI

I think you'll love the creamy and smooth texture of this soup...it's naturally sweet and savory at the same time. It's perfect accompanied by some hearty sourdough bread!

1-1/2 lbs. butternut squash,
   peeled and cubed
1 onion, quartered
1 carrot, peeled and cubed
1 sweet potato, peeled and cubed
1/2 t. sugar
1/4 t. cinnamon
1/8 t. nutmeg

1/4 t. salt
1/8 t. pepper
1/8 t. ground ginger
3 cubes chicken bouillon
3 c. water
1 c. whipping cream or
   half-and-half

Add all ingredients except cream or half-and-half to a slow cooker. Cover and cook on low setting for 8 to 10 hours, or on high setting for 4 to 5 hours. Using an immersion blender, purée squash mixture in the slow cooker, or carefully purée in batches using a blender. Return contents back to slow cooker. In a small bowl, combine cream or half-and-half with about 1/4 cup of puréed mixture. Pour cream mixture into slow cooker; mix well. Serves 4 to 6.

Turn a bowl of cream soup into spiderweb soup...eek! Spoon several tablespoons of sour cream into a plastic zipping bag. Snip off one corner and pipe the sour cream in circles on the soup. To create a web effect, pull a toothpick across the circles, starting in the center.

Spaghetti Bolognese

Chad Rutan
Gooseberry Patch

Using the slow cooker is a great way to slowly develop
the flavors of this easy-to-make meat sauce.

6 slices bacon, cut into 1/2-inch
   pieces
1 c. onion, diced
3 cloves garlic, minced
2 lbs. ground beef
4 c. spaghetti sauce
1 c. milk
16-oz. pkg. spaghetti, uncooked
Garnish: grated Parmesan
   cheese

In a skillet over medium-high heat, cook bacon until crisp. Remove
bacon from skillet and drain, reserving one tablespoon drippings. Add
onion; cook and stir until tender. Add garlic and beef; cook until beef
is well browned. Drain. To a 6-quart slow cooker, add bacon, beef
mixture, sauce and milk; stir. Cover and cook on high setting for
4 to 5 hours. About 10 minutes before serving, prepare spaghetti as
directed by package; drain. Serve sauce ladled over spaghetti; garnish
with Parmesan cheese. Serves 8.

Be sure to reheat leftovers in the microwave or on the stove.
Reheating in the slow cooker is unsafe, as it takes too long
for the food to reach the desired internal temperature.

Yummy Pizza Soup

Karen Hart
Franklin, TN

Serve with garlic bread and a tossed green salad for a complete meal.

1 lb. ground beef
1 lb. ground Italian pork
    sausage
1 onion, chopped
8-oz. pkg. sliced pepperoni
28-oz. can crushed tomatoes
2 8-oz. cans tomato sauce
4-1/4 oz. can chopped black
    olives, drained

3 cubes chicken bouillon
2 c. water
1 t. dried oregano
1 t. dried basil
1 t. garlic powder
16-oz. pkg. medium shell pasta,
    uncooked
Garnish: 2 c. shredded
    mozzarella cheese

In a large skillet over medium heat, brown beef, sausage and onion; drain. Add beef mixture and remaining ingredients except pasta and cheese to a slow cooker. Cover and cook on low setting for 4 to 6 hours. About 15 minutes before serving, cook pasta according to package directions; drain. Serve soup ladled over pasta in individual bowls; top with cheese. Serves 8 to 10.

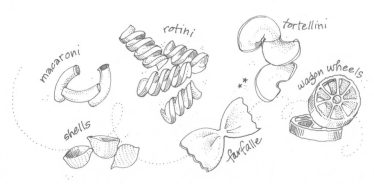

Did you know that you can cook pasta in the slow cooker? If you're adding dry pasta to a recipe, be sure the sauce is fairly watery, because the pasta will absorb a lot of the water as it cooks. Add pasta towards the end of cooking time and stir well. Serve as soon as pasta reaches desired tenderness, about 20 to 30 minutes.

Kimberly's Taco Soup

Kimberly Adams
Tacoma, WA

*I created this recipe on a cold fall day. It's perfect if you
love tacos but want something warm and comforting!*

1 lb. ground pork sausage
1 lb. ground beef
1 yellow onion, diced
2 14-1/2 oz. cans diced
    tomatoes
2 15-oz. cans black beans,
    drained and rinsed
2 15-oz. cans red beans,
    drained and rinsed

10-3/4 oz. can tomato soup
4 to 6 c. water
2 t. dried oregano
2 t. ground cumin
2 t. garlic powder
salt, pepper and cayenne pepper
    to taste
Garnish: sour cream, tortilla
    chips

In a large skillet over medium heat, brown sausage and beef; add
onion. Cook and stir until meat is no longer pink and onion is tender;
drain. Transfer mixture to a slow cooker. Add tomatoes with juice and
remaining ingredients except garnish. Cover and cook on low setting
for 4 to 6 hours. Garnish individual servings with sour cream and
tortilla chips. Serves 6 to 8.

A soup supper menu doesn't need to be fussy, and the serving
style is "help yourself!" A variety of soups kept warm in
slow cookers, along with some rolls and a crock of creamery
butter, is all that's needed. No kitchen duty at this gathering...
just relax and enjoy each other's company.

Fajita Rice Bowls

Kristin Turner
Fuquay-Varina, NC

My husband loves Tex Mex-inspired food, but he's a very picky eater. I devised this recipe by combining a couple of recipes that featured his favorite things. It's perfect for a crisp fall evening.

1 lb. ground beef
salt and pepper to taste
1 onion, chopped
1 green pepper, chopped
1/4 to 1/2 c. chipotle-lime
   marinade

16-oz. can crushed tomatoes
8-oz. can tomato sauce
1 c. beef broth
cooked rice
Garnish: sour cream, shredded
   cheese, tortilla chips

In a skillet over medium heat, brown beef with salt and pepper; drain. Place beef in a slow cooker. In the same skillet, sauté onion and green pepper in marinade for 5 minutes, or until tender. Add to slow cooker; pour in tomatoes with juice, tomato sauce and broth. Season with more salt and pepper, if desired. Cover and cook on low setting for 2 to 4 hours, until heated through. Serve over rice; top with sour cream, cheese and tortilla chips, if desired. Serves 2 to 4.

If you're buying ground beef or turkey in large quantities, why not use your slow cooker to brown it all at once? It will be ready for recipes whenever you need it! Just add up to 5 pounds of freshly ground meat to a large slow cooker; add some chopped onion if desired. Cover and cook on high setting for 2 to 2-1/2 hours, or until brown, stirring every so often. Drain in a colander; cool and divide into freezer-ready portions.

Crockery Chicken Parmigiana

Diane Tracy
Lake Mary, FL

This chicken is incredibly delicious and so tender you won't need a knife. Everyone is incredulous...chicken parmigiana in the slow cooker? Then they try it and they are sold!

1 egg
1/2 c. milk
salt and pepper to taste
1 to 1-1/2 c. Italian-flavored dry
   bread crumbs
1/2 t. garlic powder
1/2 t. dried oregano
1/2 t. dried basil
4 boneless, skinless chicken
   breasts
2 T. oil
26-oz. jar spaghetti sauce,
   divided
1 c. shredded mozzarella cheese

Whisk together egg and milk in a shallow bowl; sprinkle with salt and pepper. In a separate shallow bowl, combine bread crumbs and seasonings. Dip each piece of chicken in egg mixture, then dredge in bread crumb mixture until well coated. In a skillet over medium heat, brown chicken in oil until crust is deeply golden. Do not cook through. Spread one cup sauce in a slow cooker; add chicken. Top with remaining sauce. Cover and cook on low setting for 6 to 8 hours. About 15 minutes before serving, sprinkle with cheese. Cover and cook on low setting for 15 minutes, or until cheese melts. Serves 4.

A spine-chilling accent for your Halloween party punch bowl.
Fill a plastic surgical glove with water; tie tightly and freeze.
Remove from glove to reveal an icy, ghostly hand.

ABC Meatloaf

Lauren Williams
Kewanee, MO

This is the only meatloaf that my family will eat. It's fun to use the alphabet vegetable soup!

1-1/2 lbs. ground beef chuck
10-1/2 oz. can vegetarian
   vegetable soup
1 egg, lightly beaten

1 c. old-fashioned oats,
   uncooked
salt and pepper to taste

In a bowl, combine all ingredients until well blended. Shape mixture into a flattened loaf. Place in a lightly greased slow cooker. Cover and cook on low setting for 8 hours. Serves 4 to 6.

Easy Veggie-Beef Soup

Sara Huntley
Dodge Center, MN

I've been making this soup in the slow cooker since my kids were little! Serve with warm biscuits for a comforting meal on a chilly night.

1 lb. beef chuck roast, cut into
   bite-size pieces
16-oz. pkg. frozen soup
   vegetables
3 to 4 potatoes, peeled and
   cubed

1/2 lb. baby carrots, cut into
   bite-size pieces
4 c. beef broth

Combine all ingredients in a slow cooker. Cover and cook on low setting for 8 to 10 hours. Serves 10.

Enchilada Bake

Laurie Harris
College Station, TX

*This recipe is perfect for busy nights when my family eats
at different times. The enchiladas stay hot and ready
in the slow cooker...no need to reheat!*

1 lb. lean ground beef
1/2 c. onion, chopped
1 green pepper, chopped
1 T. oil
15-oz. can ranch-style beans,
  drained
10-oz. can mild diced tomatoes
  with green chiles, drained
1 t. chili powder

1/2 t. ground cumin
1/2 t. salt
1/4 t. pepper
1/4 t. garlic powder
8 flour tortillas
2 c. shredded Colby Jack cheese,
  divided
15-oz. can red enchilada sauce

In a skillet over medium heat, brown beef; drain. Transfer beef to a
large bowl. In the same skillet, sauté onion and pepper in oil until
tender; drain and add to beef. Add beans, tomatoes and seasonings to
beef mixture; mix well. In a slow cooker, place 2 tortillas side-by-side,
overlapping if necessary. Top evenly with 1/4 of beef mixture and
1/2 cup of cheese. Repeat layers 3 times. Pour enchilada sauce over
top. Cover and cook on low setting for 2 to 2-1/2 hours, until heated
through. Serves 8.

Still too warm for a fire? Give your fireplace a welcoming
autumn glow...fill it with pots of flame-colored
orange and yellow mums.

Slow-Cooker Spanish Rice

Wendy Ramsey
Alliance, OH

*It's hard to imagine how this tasty rice could be
any easier to make!*

2 lbs. ground beef
2 14-1/2 oz. cans petite diced
    tomatoes
1 onion, chopped

1 green pepper, chopped
29-oz. can tomato sauce
1 c. instant rice, uncooked

In a large skillet over medium heat, brown beef; drain. Place beef,
tomatoes with juice and remaining ingredients in a slow cooker. Stir
well. Cover and cook on high setting for 3 hours, or until rice is tender.
Stir in a little bit of water if rice seems too dry. Serves 8 to 10.

Don't overfill your slow cooker...it should be one-half to
two-thirds full. If it's too full, it will take too long to start
simmering. If it's not full enough, the food may be overcooked.

Un-Chili

Tara Horton
Delaware, OH

My family really enjoys my chili recipe made with red beans and tomato sauce. To make it more special, the first pot of chili for the season is always served on October 1st and the last hurrah is Opening Day for the Cincinnati Reds. One September, we had a hankering for my chili, but I wasn't allowed to make it yet...so this slightly different "un-chili" recipe was created!

1 lb. ground beef
1 clove garlic, minced
14-1/2 oz. can black beans,
    drained and rinsed
1 c. beef broth
14-1/2 oz. can petite diced
    tomatoes
1/4 t. sugar

1 T. chili powder
1-1/2 t. cumin
salt and pepper to taste
1/4 to 1/2 c. water
1/4 c. frozen corn
Garnish: shredded Cheddar
    cheese, corn chips

In a skillet over medium heat, cook beef until almost browned. Add garlic and stir until beef is cooked through; drain. In a slow cooker, combine beef mixture, beans, broth, tomatoes with juice, sugar, seasonings and water. Cover and cook on high setting for 2 hours, or on low setting for 4 hours. Stir in corn for the last 15 minutes of cooking time. Garnish as desired. Serves 4 to 6.

Instead of soaking, dried beans can be slow-cooked overnight on low. Cover with water and add a teaspoon of baking soda. In the morning, simply drain and they're ready to use.

Pumpkin & Black Bean Chili

Michèle Tungett
Rochester, IL

This unusual dish has become a family-favorite recipe. The kids especially love it! The addition of pumpkin may sound strange at first, but no one even knows it's there unless you tell them.

1 to 2 T. olive oil
1 lb. ground turkey
1 yellow onion, diced
3 cloves garlic, minced
14-1/2 oz. can diced tomatoes
    with green chiles
3 c. low-sodium chicken broth
2 15-oz. cans black beans,
    drained and rinsed

15-oz. can pumpkin
2 t. chili powder
2 t. dried parsley
1-1/2 t. dried oregano
1-1/2 t. ground cumin
1/4 t. paprika
1/4 t. salt
1/4 t. pepper

Heat oil in a skillet over medium heat. Brown turkey with onion and garlic until fully cooked; drain if needed. Add turkey mixture to a 5-quart slow cooker; stir in tomatoes with juice and remaining ingredients. Cover and cook on low setting for 4 to 5 hours. Serves 8 to 10.

If there seems to be a bit too much liquid inside the slow cooker and it's almost dinnertime, tilt the lid and turn the slow cooker to its high setting. Soon the liquid will begin to evaporate.

One-Pot Chicken & Dressing

Debbie Moore
Fort Worth, TX

This recipe is a long-time favorite in our house for Sunday lunch. Upon our return from church, our two little girls always close their eyes, inhale deeply and say, "Mmm. It smells like Thanksgiving."

2 T. butter
1/2 c. onion, diced
2 stalks celery, diced
10-3/4 oz. cream of chicken
   soup
14-1/2 oz. can chicken broth

1 c. water
2 6-oz. pkgs. stuffing mix
3 to 4-lb. herb-seasoned deli
   roast chicken, boned
   and cubed

In a skillet over medium heat, combine butter, onion and celery. Cook and stir until onion becomes translucent; set aside. In a large bowl, combine soup, broth and water. Stir in dry stuffing mix, onion mixture and chicken. Mix well. Transfer to a slow cooker. Cover and cook on low setting for 3 to 4 hours. Serves 4 to 6.

Do you have lots of leftover turkey? It freezes well for up to three months. Cut turkey into bite-size pieces, place in plastic freezer bags and pop in the freezer...ready to stir into hearty casseroles or soups whenever you are!

Potato Puff Casserole

Jennifer Knouse
New Oxford, PA

This a great meal for activity-filled school nights...I load up the slow cooker before the kids get home from school. Then, off to sports practices and scout meetings. Finally, back home to a hot meal!

1 lb. ground beef or turkey
10-3/4 oz. can cream of
   mushroom soup
1/4 c. milk
1 T. dried, minced onion
1/2 t. salt

1/4 t. pepper
2 14-1/2 oz. cans cut green
   beans, drained
32-oz. pkg. frozen potato puffs
Garnish: shredded Cheddar
   cheese

In a large skillet over medium heat, brown meat; drain. Add remaining ingredients except potato puffs and garnish; mix well. Line a slow cooker with frozen potato puffs. Spread meat mixture over potatoes. Cover and cook on high setting for 3 hours. Sprinkle individual servings with cheese. Serves 6.

Buttery Mushrooms

Wendy Wright
New London, WI

My family loves these buttery one-bite mushrooms! So simple and easy. We serve them at all of our get-togethers.

16-oz. pkg. whole mushrooms
1/2 c. butter, melted

1-oz. pkg. ranch salad dressing
   mix

Place mushrooms in a 3-1/2 qt. slow cooker. In a small bowl, whisk together butter and salad dressing mix. Pour over mushrooms. Cover and cook on low setting for 3 hours. Serves 6.

Camper's Chicken Chili

Carolyn Deckard
Bedford, IN

This is a nice cool-weather soup to fix when we are camping in the fall. Last year I won the campground-wide chili cook-off with this recipe!

2 14-1/2 oz. cans stewed
   tomatoes with garlic and
   onions
2 15-oz. cans pinto beans
10-oz. can enchilada sauce
1-3/4 lbs. boneless, skinless
   chicken breasts

1 onion, chopped
2 stalks celery, sliced
2 t. chili powder
1 t. ground cumin
Garnish: scoop-style corn chips,
   sour cream, chopped fresh
   cilantro

Spray a 4 to 5-quart slow cooker with non-stick vegetable spray. Pour in tomatoes with juice and beans with liquid; add remaining ingredients except garnish. Cover and cook on low setting for 7 to 8 hours. Shred chicken with 2 forks; stir into mixture in slow cooker. Garnish individual servings as desired. Serves 6 to 8.

Bake up some ice cream cone cupcakes for a back-to-school party. Prepare a cake mix and fill 24 flat-bottom cones 2/3 full of batter. Set the cones in muffin tins and bake as package directs for cupcakes. Cool, then add frosting and lots of candy sprinkles.

Creamy Corn Pudding

Diane Tibbott
Northern Cambria, PA

Warm and delicious...a perfect addition to a ham, chicken or turkey dinner in our house.

8-oz. pkg. cream cheese,
   softened
2 eggs, beaten
1/2 c. sugar
8-1/2 oz. pkg. corn muffin mix
2-1/2 c. frozen corn

16-oz. can creamed corn
1 c. milk
2 T. butter, melted
1 t. seasoned salt
1/4 t. nutmeg

Lightly grease a slow cooker. In a bowl, blend cream cheese, eggs and sugar. Stir in dry muffin mix and remaining ingredients; mix well. Transfer mixture to slow cooker. Cover and cook on high setting for 3 to 4 hours. Serves 8.

A hollowed-out pumpkin makes a fun flower vase...try other hard winter squashes too! Cut an opening at the top of the squash and slip in a small plastic cup or a floral tube. Fill with flowers and add water to keep them fresh.

Slow-Cooker Turkey

Margo Sloan
Ontario, Canada

*I made this for the first time last winter...it was so nice
to come home to!*

1 T. oil
1 onion, chopped
2 T. apple jelly
6-oz. pkg. stuffing mix

3/4 c. water
2-lb. boneless, skinless turkey
  breast
salt and pepper to taste

Heat oil in a skillet over medium heat. Add onion and cook, stirring frequently, for 5 minutes, or until golden. Add jelly; cook and stir for one minute longer. Spray a 4 to 6-quart slow cooker with non-stick vegetable spray. Add dry stuffing mix; drizzle with water and stir to moisten. Sprinkle turkey with salt and pepper; place on top of stuffing mix. Spoon onion mixture over turkey. Cover and cook on low setting for 5 to 6 hours, until turkey juices run clear when pierced. Serves 4.

Put a slow cooker to work turning the leftovers of the holiday bird into flavorful broth for soup. Place the bones in a large slow cooker, breaking to fit if necessary. Add onion, celery, carrots and enough water to fill 2/3 full. Cover and cook on low for about 10 hours. Strain broth with a colander and refrigerate or freeze.

Homestyle Stuffing

Lori Rosenberg
University Heights, OH

*Honestly, this stuffing recipe tastes just like the one my mom
used to make...but she spent hours fussing over hers!*

2 c. celery, chopped
2 c. onion, chopped
1/4 c. fresh parsley, minced
1 T. margarine
24-oz. pkg. bread cubes for
    stuffing
1-1/2 t. salt

1-1/2 t. dried sage
1 t. poultry seasoning
1/2 t. dried thyme
1/2 t. seasoned salt
1/2 t. pepper
2 eggs, well beaten
32-oz. container chicken broth

In a large skillet over medium heat, sauté celery, onion and parsley in
margarine until vegetables are tender. In a large bowl, toss together
bread cubes and seasonings. In a small bowl, whisk together eggs and
broth; pour over bread mixture. Add celery mixture; mix well. Transfer
to a greased slow cooker. Cover and cook on low setting for 5 hours.
Serves 10 to 12.

Start a Thanksgiving tradition! Lay a blank card on each
dinner plate and invite guests to write down what they are
most thankful for this year. Later, bind the cards together
with a ribbon to create a sweet gratitude book.

Apple Cider Pork Chops

Vicki Walsh
Kansas City, MO

This recipe has become a favorite of ours, especially in the fall.
It makes the whole house smell of apples and cinnamon.

4 to 6 thin pork chops
1 c. chicken broth
2 c. apple cider or apple juice
1/4 t. celery seed

1/4 c. brown sugar, packed
1 t. cinnamon
1 apple, sliced

Arrange pork chops in a single layer in a slow cooker. Pour broth over chops. Add apple cider or juice; sprinkle with celery seed. Cover and cook on low setting for 5 to 6 hours, until chops are tender. Add brown sugar, cinnamon and apple. Cover and cook on high setting for 30 to 45 minutes longer. Makes 4 servings.

For an easy Thanksgiving centerpiece, pile Jack-be-Little and Baby Boo pumpkins along with acorn and dumpling squash on your favorite cake stand.

Sweet Potato Casserole

Bethi Hendrickson
Danville, PA

This yummy dish is a must for any fall brunch!

6 c. sweet potatoes, cooked and
    mashed
1/3 c. butter, melted
2 T. sugar
3 T. brown sugar, packed
1 T. orange juice

2 eggs, beaten
1/2 c. fat-free half-and-half
    or milk
2 t. cinnamon
1 t. nutmeg

In a large bowl, blend potatoes, butter and sugars. Stir in remaining ingredients. Transfer mixture to a lightly greased slow cooker, spreading evenly. Spoon Pecan Topping evenly over top, pressing down lightly. Cover and cook on high setting for 3 to 4 hours. Serves 8.

Pecan Topping:

1/3 c. chopped pecans, toasted
1/3 c. brown sugar, packed

2 T. all-purpose flour
2 T. butter, melted

In a bowl, combine all ingredients.

Show your spirit...dress up
a garden scarecrow in a
hometown football jersey.
Go Team!

Cranberry Pork Roast

Debbie Blundi
Kunkletown, PA

I love to cook and try new things. I have a captive audience in my husband, who loves to eat and is more than willing to taste-test anything I make. This pork roast was a winner!

1-1/2 to 2-lb. boneless pork roast
16-oz. can whole-berry cranberry sauce
2 16-oz. cans diced pears in light syrup
1-1/2 oz. pkg. beef stew seasoning mix
Optional: 1 to 2 T. cornstarch

Place pork in a 5 to 7-quart slow cooker; add remaining ingredients except cornstarch. Cover and cook on high setting for 6 to 8 hours. Remove pork from slow cooker. If desired, add cornstarch to drippings left in the slow cooker to make gravy; whisk well and cook until thickened. Serves 4 to 6.

Apple Pie Pork Roast

Georgianne Keenan
Chino, CA

This is a quick & easy four-ingredient recipe that everyone loves!

4-lb. boneless pork roast
2 21-oz. cans apple pie filling
1 onion, chopped
1/2 c. butter, sliced

Place pork roast in a large slow cooker that has been sprayed with non-stick vegetable spray. Pour pie filling over roast; sprinkle with onion. Dot with butter. Cover and cook on high setting for 8 hours, or until pork is tender and no longer pink in the center. Serves 8.

Get a head start on holiday festivities! Soon after the leaves begin to fall, check your local newspaper or city's website for once-a-year events like craft bazaars, storytelling, caroling and the lighting of the Christmas tree in Town Square.

Spicy Sweet Potatoes

Vickie

*Looking for something a little different this Thanksgiving?
Your guests will be pleasantly surprised by these
sweet potatoes with a little kick!*

1/3 c. oil
1/4 c. brown sugar, packed
2 t. chili powder
1/4 t. chipotle chili powder

1/4 t. salt
3 lbs. sweet potatoes, peeled and
   cut into large chunks

In a large bowl, combine oil, brown sugar and seasonings; add sweet potatoes and toss to coat. Transfer to a 6-quart slow cooker. Cover and cook on high setting for 2 to 3 hours, until potatoes are tender and golden. Serves 4 to 6.

Not what we say about our blessings,
but how we use them, is the true
measure of our thanksgiving.

–W.T. Purkiser

Best Canadian Turkey Stuffing

Lorna MacDonald
Ontario, Canada

*My turkey stuffing is a hit at every Thanksgiving and
Christmas dinner...and it's made in a slow cooker!*

1 loaf sourdough bread, cubed
1 loaf whole-grain bread, cubed
1 loaf raisin bread, cubed
poultry seasoning, salt and
    pepper to taste

1 sweet onion, diced
3 stalks celery, diced
8-oz. pkg. sliced mushrooms
1/4 c. butter
1 c. sweetened dried cranberries

The day before preparing stuffing, place bread cubes in a very large
roasting pan; season generously with poultry seasoning, salt and
pepper. Toss every few hours, until bread is dry. In a large skillet,
sauté onion, celery and mushrooms in butter until tender. Stir in
cranberries; pour in Giblet Broth. Stir well. Remove from heat; cool.
Pour Giblet Broth mixture over bread cubes, a little at a time; mix
thoroughly, until just moistened. Place bread mixture in a large slow
cooker. Cover and cook on low setting for 3 to 4 hours, stirring
occasionally. Serves 18 to 20.

Giblet Broth:

turkey giblets

32-oz. container chicken broth

Place giblets in a saucepan, cover with water and bring to a boil.
Reduce heat; simmer 2 hours. Remove giblets from saucepan. Remove
any bones or skin; chop meat and return to water in saucepan. Add
chicken broth; return to a simmer.

Paperwhite narcissus bulbs are easy to plant
and fast-growing too! Plant four to six weeks
before Christmas and you'll enjoy their
tiny white flowers on your holiday table.

Cinnamon-Cranberry Applesauce

Suzanne Satterlee
Oak Park, IL

Homemade applesauce is one of my favorite comfort foods. It's easy. It's healthy. It fills my home with lovely autumnal aromas while cooking. And it's inexpensive, but feels fancy and tastes rich...in fact, we usually have it for dessert!

5 to 6 apples, peeled, cored and
   coarsely chopped
1 T. lemon juice
1/4 c. water
1 t. vanilla extract

1/2 t. cinnamon
1 T. brown sugar, packed
1/4 c. sweetened dried
   cranberries

Place apples in a 3-1/2 to 4-quart slow cooker. Add remaining ingredients except cranberries; stir to combine. Cover and cook on low setting for 4 to 6 hours, until apples are fork-tender. Mash apples; stir in cranberries. Cover and cook on low setting for 15 to 30 minutes longer, until cranberries are plumped. Serve warm or cold. Serves 4 to 5.

Fill a bushel basket with a jar of Cinnamon-Cranberry Applesauce, a gallon of cider and fresh-baked scones... give to a friend to help celebrate autumn.

Hearty Harvest Favorites

Girl Scout Apples

Jackie Garvin
Valrico, FL

Baked apples have always been "Girl Scout apples" to me, because I learned to make them in Girl Scouts, just like I did Toad-in-the-Hole. Out of all the activities we did in Girl Scouts, the cooking memories have stayed with me the most.

1/2 c. brown sugar, packed
1/2 c. butter, softened
1 t. cinnamon
1/2 t. vanilla extract
Optional: 2 to 3 drops lemon
    extract

1-1/2 oz. pkg. raisins
4 Granny Smith apples, cored
    with stem ends reserved

In a bowl, combine all ingredients except apples. Stuff each apple with 1/4 of the brown sugar mixture. Plug the stem end back in. Place apples upright in a slow cooker. Cover and cook on high setting for 3 to 4 hours, until apples are tender but not falling apart. Makes 4 servings.

Crispy Rice Treats

Lori Rosenburg
University Heights, OH

This recipe yields the same great results as the traditional method of making crispy rice bars, but with a lot less mess in the kitchen, which makes it a winner in my book!

3 T. butter, sliced
4 c. mini marshmallows

6 c. crispy rice cereal

Place butter in a slow cooker; add marshmallows and cereal. Cover and cook on high setting for one hour. Stir well. If needed, cover and cook for 15 to 20 minutes longer, until marshmallows are fully melted. Butter a 11"x9" glass baking pan. Transfer mixture from slow cooker to baking pan; press mixture firmly into pan, using a buttered spatula or your hands. Cool; cut into squares. Serves 12.

Pumpkin Butter

Laura Williams
Evensville, TN

My husband calls this "Pumpkin Pie in a Jar." If you don't have fresh pumpkin, you can substitute a 15-ounce can of pumpkin. You can easily double or triple this recipe. It's wonderful to keep on hand for making homemade pumpkin pies or bread.

2 c. fresh pumpkin, cooked and puréed	1/4 t. nutmeg
1 c. sugar	1/2 t. ginger
1 c. brown sugar, packed	1/8 t. ground cloves
1 t. cinnamon	4 1/2-pint canning jars and lids, sterilized

Combine all ingredients in a slow cooker; mix well. Cover and cook on high setting for 3 hours, stirring occasionally to prevent scorching. It will thicken as it cooks. Ladle hot mixture into hot sterilized jars, leaving 1/4-inch headspace. Wipe rims; secure with lids and rings. Process in a boiling water bath for 40 minutes or pressure canner at 10 pounds of pressure for 20 minutes. Set jars on a towel to cool; check for seals. Makes about four 1/2-pint jars.

Pumpkin Butter Pies:

3 1/2-pt. jars Pumpkin Butter	12-oz. can evaporated milk
2 eggs, beaten	2 9-inch pie crusts

Combine pumpkin butter, eggs and milk. Divide mixture between two 9" pie crusts. Bake, uncovered, at 425 degrees for 15 minutes; reduce heat to 350 degrees and bake for 45 minutes longer, or until pies test done. Makes 2 pies.

Old quilts, buffalo check blankets and blanket-stitched throws make the best spreads for an outdoor autumn picnic or tailgating party!

Pumpkin Pie Pudding

Hollie Moots
Marysville, OH

You can garnish individual bowls of this delicious dessert with crumbled gingersnap cookies or baked pie crust cut-outs...yum! This pie is so simple to put together and makes the house smell wonderful while it cooks.

15-oz. can pumpkin
12-oz. can evaporated milk
3/4 c. brown sugar, packed
1/2 c. all-purpose flour
1/4 t. salt

1/2 t. baking powder
2 eggs, beaten
2 T. butter, melted
2 t. pumpkin pie spice
Garnish: whipped cream

In a bowl, combine all ingredients except garnish; mix well. Transfer to a 3 to 4-quart slow cooker that has been sprayed with non-stick vegetable spray. Cover and cook on low setting for 4 to 6 hours, until set. Serve warm or cooled, spooned into bowls and garnished as desired. Serves 6 to 8.

It's easy to make pie crust garnishes! Just use tiny cookie cutters to cut shapes from a homemade or store-bought pie crust. Arrange cut-outs on a baking sheet lined with parchment paper. Lightly spritz with non-stick vegetable spray and sprinkle with cinnamon. Bake at 350 degrees for about 6 minutes, or until golden. Cool.

Slow-Cooker Apple Pie

Diana Krol
Nickerson, KS

This is a wonderful dessert to take to potluck dinners or tailgating parties...especially in the fall when the apples are at their peak.

8 c. apples, peeled, cored
 and sliced
1-1/4 t. cinnamon
1/4 t. nutmeg
2 eggs, beaten
3/4 c. milk
2 t. vanilla extract

3/4 c. sugar
5 T. butter, softened and divided
1-1/2 c. biscuit baking mix,
 divided
1/3 c. brown sugar, packed
Garnish: whipped cream or
 vanilla ice cream

In a large bowl, toss together apples, cinnamon and nutmeg; transfer to a greased slow cooker. In a bowl, blend eggs, milk, vanilla, sugar, 2 tablespoons butter and 3/4 cup baking mix. Spoon batter over apples. In a small bowl, combine brown sugar and remaining baking mix; cut in remaining butter until mixture resembles coarse crumbs. Spoon brown sugar mixture over batter. Do not stir. Cover and cook on low setting for 6 to 7 hours. Serve warm, spooned into individual bowls and topped with whipped cream or ice cream. Serves 8 to 10.

Make a trip to the apple orchard a family event this year. You'll bring home baskets of crisp apples and jugs of tangy apple cider...perfect for fall slow cooking.

Cinnamon-Raisin Bread Pudding

Terri Kearney
Maple Hill, NC

My husband, my best friend and my mother-in-law can all agree on on one thing...they love this warm and hearty bread pudding!

4 c. cinnamon-raisin bread,
   toasted and cubed
2 eggs
3/4 c. sugar
2-1/2 c. milk, heated to boiling
   and cooled

2 T. butter, melted
1 t. vanilla extract
1/8 t. nutmeg
1/8 t. salt
Garnish: whipped cream

Add bread cubes to a slow cooker that has been sprayed with non-stick vegetable spray. In a bowl, beat eggs and sugar; whisk in remaining ingredients except garnish. Pour over bread cubes, mixing well and pressing down so bread will soak up milk mixture. Cover and cook on low setting for 6 hours. Spoon into individual bowls; serve warm topped with whipped cream. Makes 8 servings.

Bread pudding is a scrumptious way to use up day-old bread.
Try French bread, raisin bread or even left over cinnamon
buns or doughnuts for an extra-tasty dessert!

Apple Spice Cake

Angie McCabe
Monticello, IL

*Warm apple spice cake makes the whole house smell like
grandma's kitchen on a cold fall day...mmm!*

21-oz. can apple pie filling
18-1/4 oz. pkg. spice cake mix

1/2 c. butter
Garnish: vanilla ice cream

Spray a slow cooker generously with non-stick vegetable spray. Spread
pie filling in slow cooker; sprinkle evenly with dry cake mix. Do not
stir. Dot with butter. Cover and cook on high setting for 2 to 3 hours,
until center has risen and edges are bubbly. Spoon into individual
bowls; serve warm, topped with ice cream. Serves 8.

Celebrate Johnny Appleseed's birthday on September 26...
it's a tasty reason to enjoy an apple treat of any kind!

Index

Index

Index

Have a taste for more?

We created our official Circle of Friends so we could
fill everyone in on the latest scoop at once.
Visit us online to join in the fun and discover free
recipes, exclusive giveaways and much more!

www.gooseberrypatch.com

Call us toll-free at 1·800·854·6673

U.S. to Canadian recipe equivalents

Volume Measurements

1/4 teaspoon	1 mL
1/2 teaspoon	2 mL
1 teaspoon	5 mL
1 tablespoon = 3 teaspoons	15 mL
2 tablespoons = 1 fluid ounce	30 mL
1/4 cup	60 mL
1/3 cup	75 mL
1/2 cup = 4 fluid ounces	125 mL
1 cup = 8 fluid ounces	250 mL
2 cups = 1 pint =16 fluid ounces	500 mL
4 cups = 1 quart	1 L

Weights

1 ounce	30 g
4 ounces	120 g
8 ounces	225 g
16 ounces = 1 pound	450 g

Oven Temperatures

300° F	150° C
325° F	160° C
350° F	180° C
375° F	190° C
400° F	200° C
450° F	230° C

Baking Pan Sizes

Square

8x8x2 inches	2 L = 20x20x5 cm
9x9x2 inches	2.5 L = 23x23x5 cm

Rectangular

13x9x2 inches	3.5 L = 33x23x5 cm

Loaf

9x5x3 inches	2 L = 23x13x7 cm

Round

8x1-1/2 inches	1.2 L = 20x4 cm
9x1-1/2 inches	1.5 L = 23x4 cm